HOW TO
RUN A RV DEALERSHIP

22 Best Kept Secrets to Help You Run Your Dealership

Marco A. Martinez

D1113158

THIS SERIES OF HELPFUL DEALERSHIP
ARTICLES IS PRESENTED TO YOU BY:
Marco A. Martinez, President
Best Friends Consulting, Inc.
www.BestFriendsConsulting.com

Serving the Needs of the RV/Marine/Auto Dealership Family
Marco A. Martinez, Consultant
Marco@bestfriendsconsulting.com

Best Friends Consulting, Inc.
2nd Edition July 2013

ISBN: 1490996680
ISBN-13: 978-1490996684

Cover artwork by Skillful Antics - www.skillfulantics.com

HOW TO
RUN A RV DEALERSHIP

22 Best Kept Secrets to Help You Run Your Dealership

Marco A. Martinez

DEDICATION

I wish to dedicate this helpful resource booklet to all my friends in the dealership world who have shared their operational knowledge with me throughout the many years of my involvement with them. Most of my knowledge has come from 'old-timers' who own their own dealership and have eagerly sought to improve their operations and profit margins though further learning.

My hope is that at least one article in this booklet will help those who read this publication and thereby make your dealership operations more effective. Enjoy your reading and remember, Best Friends Consulting is always available to answer further questions you may have regarding your dealership operations.

Marco A. Martinez
352-239-7697
Marco@BestFriendsConsulting.com

CONTENTS

CHAPTER I

GET YOUR DEALERSHIP ORGANIZED ON PAPER

Don't Assume Everyone Knows Each Other's Roles.

When I first started serving various dealerships as a VP of RV manufacturing, I discovered that it was very hard over the telephone to determine who exactly was in charge. I could always speak directly to the owner of the RV dealership - he or she knew they were in charge. However, when the owner was absent, everyone from sales staff members to the service manager claimed to be in charge of the dealership. When I went into the retail side of the RV world, it confirmed the reality that dealerships often fail to establish clear-cut lines of authority and responsibility in their dealership. The main reason for this was the management's fear that certain key people in the organization might be offended if their name were placed on an organizational chart under someone else's authority (other than the owners). Service managers, parts managers, warranty managers, sales managers, and even accounting managers/controllers often feel that no one other than the owners are over them in authority. This may be a good philosophy when you first start an RV business, but let me tell you here and now, "this dog won't hunt!"

Each and every dealership needs to put in writing a clear chain of authority. This will organize your dealership and place a clear picture of who is responsible for certain departments. An organizational chart will help new employees to understand how they and others fit into the scheme of things. Manufacturers and vendors will appreciate knowing this information also, as it will enhance their knowledge of your dealership operations. Sometimes a vendor will be shocked to learn that the person he thought was a key member of management ended up being the parts back counter person. Every department should have a copy of the company's organizational chart clearly posted for all employees to review. If openings exist in your organization, the chart can contain a statement such as "future new position" or "position available" to alert others in the dealership to the possibility of moving into a new slot. It amazes me how dealerships often recruit an outside individual for a new job opening without first announcing the job opening to current employees. Organizational charts also help you to see the overall personnel picture and you can quickly identify both overages and shortages in your employment.

No Organization Equals CONFUSION and HEARTACHE for Owners (or GMs)

Now let me list the "stinkin' thinkin'" that results when you don't implement a chain of authority and responsibility at your dealership.

1.   Employees believe that the owners (or GM) are responsible for everything, so any problems should be given to the owners. When the owners (or GM) are absent, no one needs to resolve problems - just wait until the owners get back and blast them with all the problems at one time.

2. Lower management employees believe that they don't really have to listen to middle managers; they can go straight to the top with complaints and issues involving their departments.

3. If something goes wrong or an employee commits an error, the owners (or GM) need to come up with solutions.

4. Everyone has the authority to purchase assets on behalf of the company because no one questions their authority.

5. Employees believe that discipline is the responsibility of the owners (or GM) because all of the employees work directly for them.

I think you can see from the above list that defining and documenting a clear-cut line of authority for employees is absolutely essential. You need to have both an organizational chart and job descriptions at your dealership. Employees need to know what is expected of them and where they fit into the scheme of the dealership's total picture.

CHAPTER II

DEALERSHIP OPERATIONAL CHECKLIST

Before you "Inspect What You Expect," First Let Your Employees Know What You Expect of Them.

What is missing in the old saying - Inspect What You Expect?

When I first joined the Air Force in 1976, I was assigned to the base billeting office as a billeting clerk. My job was to ensure that authorized individuals had a place to stay in our on-base hotel-like accommodations. After six months of service, I was promoted to the base billeting accounting clerk (they love long titles in the Air Force - I think the Air Force thinks it makes up for the low pay). In this position I was told that the money had to all be accounted for on a daily basis and that a shortage of cash or theft could result in jail time. I also was told that a team of inspectors would come in and inspect my work at least once a year. These inspectors were feared by all and were known as the IG Team (Inspector General). The IG Team traveled from base to base with representatives who were experts in their fields - they knew what they were looking for! They were feared because a rating of "unsatisfactory" by them would mean that someone's head would roll. When I asked my supervisor what criteria they would use to evaluate me, she responded by saying, "checklists!" I then asked her, "what checklist?" I then found out that there were universal standard Air Force checklists that ask specific questions relating to my field of work. These checklists clearly spelled out what was expected of my department. If you used these checklists in the daily performance of your duties, you didn't need to fear the IG team. Well, guess what I did? I secured a copy of the checklist used for my department and followed the checklist! When the IG team did arrive to inspect my work, I always received outstanding ratings. It was not difficult; I just did what was expected of me. But I knew what was expected of me by first reading and knowing the checklist.

It wasn't too long ago that I met a quality inspector for Northwest Airlines in Atlanta, Georgia. I asked this woman what she did for a living and she told me she was a Quality Inspector for Northwest Airlines. She told me she traveled the world inspecting various organizations to see if they were correctly performing required processes. I asked her how she could know so much about various companies that would enable her to inspect these organizations. She then told me, "We have a team of people who develop checklists for us to use in evaluating these companies."

Well, what is the bottom line to all of this? I firmly believe that in many dealerships throughout the land, owners/GMs believe that in order to get what they want, they must "inspect what they expect!" This however doesn't work a great deal of the time because they have not written down and reviewed key areas of responsibilities with key employees. At this point, let me provide you with a sample checklist that I developed for the RV industry, which can also be modified for the Marine industry. This sample checklist is designed to evaluate the overall operations of a dealership and is therefore broad in nature. Enjoy!

Operational Checklist – Dealership Evaluation

GENERAL MANAGER

1. Do levels of inventory (combined new/used) reflect a minimum turn ratio of at least three (4) turns yearly?
2. Does the general manager maintain a list of anticipated leasehold improvements and equipment purchases for the current fiscal year?
3. Does the general manager re-evaluate value of aged inventory on a monthly basis and submit such report to corporate declaring reduced values?
4. Does the GM conduct a weekly meeting in which all managers are present and given instruction and direction for the week?
5. Does the GM directly order product from manufacturer, approve such ordered invoice, and then forward order to corporate for P.O. issuance?
6. Does the GM have access to computerized reports, and does he/she understand how to generate and analyze such reports?
7. Does the GM immediately forward any and all matters of litigation (lawsuits, tax payments delinquency) to the corporate office for review?
8. Does the GM insure that a weekly physical inventory of all RVs is performed and documented?
9. Does the GM insure that the sales of new inventory maintain a minimum gross profit ratio of ten percent (10%)?
10. Does the GM insure that the sales of used inventory maintain a minimum gross profit ratio of fifteen percent (15%)?
11. Does the GM maintain a calendar listing the vacation schedule for all members of management?
12. Does the GM maintain resumes on all levels of management?
13. Does the GM weekly monitor outstanding warranty receivables and contracts in transits?

14. Does the sales department maintain an overall yearly turn ratio of at least four times on entire vehicle inventory?

15. Has the general manager established a monthly program to sell aged inventory and is such a program coordinated with the sale manager?

16. Has the general manager established a yearly budget, which includes sales projections and anticipated expenses?

17. Has the GM established a stocking strategy report, which describes selected product lines, levels of inventory, and rebate participation?

18. Has the GM established a job description for personnel under his supervision?

19. Has the GM established a training program for the sales, service, F/I, warranty, and parts departments?

20. Has the GM established an organizational chart, and do all personnel understand the store organization?

21. Has the GM placed pay plans in written format for key personnel?

22. Has the GM appointed a specific person to handle customer delivery walk-throughs and does the individual perform after-market sales?

CONTROLLER

1. Does the controller conduct a monthly audit of MSOs and used vehicle titles to insure accountability?

2. Does the controller insure all MSOs and titles are maintained in a secure location and correctly filed?

3. Does the controller insure that check requests requiring corporate approval are forwarded to corporate office for approval?

4. Does the controller insure that cash/check deposits are made on a daily basis?

5. Does the controller insure that payroll is processed on a timely basis and submitted to the corporate payroll department?

6. Does the controller insure that the payables are posted and forwarded to corporate in a timely manner?

7. Does the controller insure that transactions are posted in the correct month income was earned?

8. Does the controller maintain a list posting the dates reports are due to corporate, state agencies, or federal agencies?

9. Does the controller maintain a listing of all equipment leases?

10. Does the controller maintain a schedule of manufacturer rebates receivables indicating date due and amount of rebates?

11. Does the controller monitor contracts in transit and inform both the F/I manager and GM of delinquent payments?

12. Does the controller monitor warranty receivables and inform both the service manager and GM of delinquent payments?

13. Does the controller stay informed as to corporate policy regarding day-to-day operations, and are policies in written format?

FINANCE AND INSURANCE MANAGER

1. Does the F/I manager contact the financial institution to collect delinquent contracts in transit?

2. Does the F/I manager insure sales staff is properly trained so that paperwork arrives to F/I in the appropriate format?

3. Does the F/I manager maintain a log posting front end and back end profits, and is such a log given weekly to the GM?

4. Does the F/I manager secure signatures on sales documentation on "date of sale" as opposed to the date of delivery?

5. Does the F/I manager securing retail financing insure search is not limited to select financial institutions?

6. Has the F/I manager established a minimum ratio of 50% penetration on the sales of extended warranties, Tire Guard, and other such products?

7. Has the F/I manager notified both the GM and corporate of any direct rebates or kickbacks offered the F/I manager directly?

SALES MANAGER

1. Does the GM weekly monitor all ACV (actual cash values) places on incoming trades?

2. Does the sales manager avoid "financially pre-qualifying" customers and allow F/I manager to process all accepted deals?

3. Does the sales manager conduct daily meetings with the sales staff?

4. Does the sales manager ensure the desking of all deals?

5. Does the sales manager maintain a daily productivity report based on the volume of "UPS"?

6. Has the sales manager established a reasonable minimum customer deposit level ($500 - $1,000)?

7. Has the sales manager established a training program for the sales staff?

8. Has the sales manager scheduled and posted all manufacturers' on-site training dates?

9. Has the sales manager scheduled and posted all sales shows for the current fiscal year?

10. Has the service manager appointed a detail supervisor who monitors daily detail operations, including delivery scheduling?

SERVICE MANAGER

1. Does the service manager conduct a weekly meeting with the parts, warranty, and detail supervisors?

2. Does the service manager conduct a monthly safety inspection and briefing?

3. Does the service manager insure that each technician produces a minimum of 40 hours of flat rate work?

4. Does the service manager ensure that a weekly technician's productivity report is produced?

5. Does the service manager ensure that all R.O. tickets (internal, warranty, customer pay, sublets) are closed in a timely manner?

6. Does the service manager ensure that the service repair area is maintained in an orderly fashion and customer units are properly identified?

7. Does the service manager produce a weekly report posting total revenue produced in all service departments, including total tech hours worked?

8. Has the service manager appointed a shop foreman to oversee technicians' daily work production?

9. Has the service manager appointed an individual to inspect new unit arrivals weekly and write-up internal tickets repairs?

10. Has the service manager appointed an individual to inspect new unit arrivals weekly and write-up warranty repairs?

11. Has the service manager established an internal rate to charge the sales department (25%, 30%, and 50%)?

12. Has the service manager established the minimum gross profit margin for the combined parts/service dept. at forty five percent (45%)?

13. Has the service manager scheduled and posted vendor/manufacturer training dates for the current fiscal year?

PARTS MANAGER

1. Does the parts manager conduct a cycle count on a monthly basis, and is the report submitted to the controller?

2. Does the parts manager establish a minimum turn ratio of 6 times per year, and does the inventory reflect such stocking levels?

3. Does the parts manager have a program in which aged parts (90 days +) are returned to the vendor for proper credit?

4. Does the parts manager ensure proper maintenance of stock parts, including parts maintained in storage sheds, truck storage areas, and the like?

5. Does the parts manager ensure that money is collected in advance for customer special orders?

6. Has the parts manager implemented a program in which the receiving department quickly receives and stocks incoming orders?

7. Has the parts manager negotiated a yearly rebate with the parts vendor determined by yearly sales?

CHAPTER III

INVENTORY TURNS

How's Your Inventory Turning?

The concept of understanding the importance of inventory turns is not new, but it is an often overlooked practice in many RV/Marine/Auto dealerships. When we have a good understanding of inventory turns, it helps us to plan, organize, predict, and evaluate how our business is doing. Demonstrating this reality is our solar system. The Earth turns once approximately every 24 hours; we call it a day. The Earth turns approximately 30 times and circles the moon once; we call this a month. The Earth turns 365 times and circles the sun once; we call this a year. We use this knowledge to create calendars by which we can plan, organize, and control our lives all based on turns.

Understanding RV/Marine/Auto turns is very important to dealers also. I can't tell you how many times I have asked a General Manager or General Sales Manager to tell me how many times their inventory is turning per year just to hear them respond by saying, "I really don't know." This incredible response tells me that a little training is in order. In this issue we will discuss how to determine your turn ratio and the value of understanding the turn ratio.

Finding Your Turn Ratio

Let's begin with the basics and do this the simple way. Determining your turn ratio for any given year requires two key pieces of data: the yearly cost of goods sold (vehicles) and your average inventory on hand. You then take these two figures and divide your cost of goods sold by your inventory number. For example, Big Ticket RV in Texas sold 10 million in RVs in the year ending December 31, 2012. The cost of the RVs Big Ticket sold was 8.1 million. The amount of inventory on hand at December 31, 2012 was 3.5 million (we will assume that Big Ticket's inventory was also 3.5 million at the beginning of the year; he therefore maintains a consistent 3.5 million yearly average inventory). Now let's determine Big Ticket's turn ratio.

Cost of Goods Sold/ Avg. Inventory = Turn Ratio
$8,100,000/$3,500,000 = 2.3 times per year

Now we need to get to second base. Let's say that the owner of Big Ticket RV needs to know if new inventory is turning faster than used inventory. He first asks his GM to find out the cost of goods sold figures for new and used RVs.

The COGS for new RVs was $5,000,000 and for the used was $3,100,000 (5 + 3.1 = 8.1 million). The GM also informs the owner that the December 31, 2012 inventory report states they had $2,750,000 in new and $750,000 in used inventory. The owner pulls out his trusty calculator and concludes the following:

New - $5,000,000 / $2,750,000 = 1.8 Times per Year
Used - $3,100,000 / $750,000 = 4.1 Times per Year
Combined - $8,100,000 / $3,500,000 = 2.3 Times per Year

So how does all this information help me? The owner of Big Ticket RV analyzed his data and was amazed to discover a variety of things. He found that new inventory was only turning 1.8 times a year, which was a very poor ratio. The owner realized that he was stocking too much new inventory. He knew that on average he was able to sell about 5 million in new inventory per year on a consistent basis. He concluded that he needed to lower his new inventory on hand to from $2,750,00 to $1,250,000. This action would enable him to turn his new inventory four times a year (4 times $1,250,000 = $5 million). He would still be able to have the same new sales numbers as the prior year; however, he would realize at least four tremendous benefits: 1) the floor plan would be reduced from 2.75 million to 1.25 million, thereby lessoning floor plan liability and avoiding maxing out the line of credit; 2) new inventory would be less likely to age, and this would avoid inventory from becoming obsolete; 3) expenses in the areas of interest, insurance, and detail washings would decrease substantially; 4) product stocking would become more focused in order to consistently stock the makes and models of new items that were selling well. The owner was proud that his used inventory was turning at least four times a year. However, he wondered if he could possibly increase his used vehicle sales if he stocked just a little bit more, since used inventory was always in demand. The owner decided that he would experiment with his new idea by allowing $150,000 more in used inventory to be maintained. He hoped he could increase his sales by over $600,000 yearly (4 x $150,000 plus gross profit).

Knowing and analyzing your turns is absolutely essential to the success and profitability of any dealer. We hope this article can be helpful to some of your management team. By the way, share this article with your Parts Department – the lesson will be the same for them!

CHAPTER IV

MANAGING YOUR USED INVENTORY

A dealership's RV/Marine/Auto inventory will generate approximately 87% to 90% of all revenue dollars earned each year. How a dealer manages his or her inventory definitely determines if the year will be profitable or not. In this issue, we will focus on used inventory management.

The amount of new and used inventory varies greatly between dealerships. Some dealers focus 100% on used merchandise in order to capture higher gross profit margins (20-30% GP) and to avoid dealing with warranty issues. Other dealers maintain a new/used ratio of 60/40, 50/50, 40/60, or 25/75.

The first step in controlling either new or used inventory is to determine your stocking levels. How much inventory should you be maintaining at your dealership on a monthly basis? Accurately answering this question assumes you have done a little research and established your dealership's turn ratio. In the previous chapter, we discussed turn ratios, so please take a peek at that chapter while reading this section. Once you have established a stocking level, it serves as a benchmark for you to use in order to determine if you should be buying used inventory or selling it. Let's assume your stocking level is $3,000,000 and you only have $2,200,000 in stock. You're a buyer at this point in the game, so let's continue.

Used inventory is usually acquired as a customer trade-in, but can also be purchased through the wholesale route. When appraising a trade, a dealer should have a specific person (manager) assigned to perform appraisals. The appraisal process must be accurate and thorough, and cannot be left to inexperienced personnel. Dealers use either the NADA Recreational Vehicle Appraisal Guide or the Kelly Blue Book to determine wholesale values. The NADA book is published and released during the months of January, May, and September of each year. In performing a sample comparison between the NADA May issue and the NADA September issue, we find that units generally depreciated approximately 5.0-7.5% depending on year, make, and model.

Based on this data, when placing a value on a trade-in during the month of August, an appraisal manager should not only take into consideration current book value, condition, mileage, charges for major damages, market demand, but also the upcoming depreciation charge that will take place in September. Sometimes managers may be aware of this fact, but they choose to go ahead with the higher ACV value in order to attain a higher sales commission on the deal. Because of this reality, a member of upper management should regularly and personally audit each deal prior to the payment of commissions. Once a unit is purchased through the trade-in system, it should have internal service performed on the unit to place it into a sellable condition. This usually consists of a PDI and the performance of minor repairs. A dealer needs to establish a clear policy on what is to be charged to a unit as an internal service, and the rate the service department will charge the sales department. While some dealers charge internals at cost, other dealers mark-up the cost between departments (parts are marked-up 15% to 30% and labor may be charged at $30-$50 per hour). We do recommend the mark-up system because it forces the sales department to become conscious of each repair request as their commissions are lowered by the cost of internals. All internal charges should be added to the cost of the unit, posted on the inventory listing, and passed on to the customer. Dealerships who do mark up their internal service to the sales department must be monitored on a routine basis, as there will be a tendency for the Service Department to generate most of its revenue from internals as opposed to customer retail and warranty service.

Once the unit is prepped and ready to sell, the goal of an effective dealership is to sell it within 90 days in order to keep turning its merchandise at least four times a year (4 x 90 = 360). When your used inventory begins to age, you've reached a critical point that requires you to take action. A good practice for a dealer to establish is to sell these used units before the 120th day in order to avoid having old merchandise and dealing with write down issues. It should be noted that some dealers don't write-down aging units at all, which is a big mistake. Some dealers write down units on the twelfth month of the year, while others mark down their units on a quarterly basis. Personally, we recommend writing down your aging units at least twice a year.

CHAPTER V

DEALERSHIP PROFIT MARGINS

Do You Know Your Margins?

Knowing your margins provides you with good yard-markers with which to locate your financial position on the field of dealership play.

When you deposit money into your local bank, you want to know what interest rate you will receive on your deposit. The banker may tell you that you will receive 1% annually on your money, which means that for every $100.00 you deposit at the beginning of the year, you will receive $1.00 at the end of the year. The 1% figure helps you understand exactly what to expect of the bank in exchange for the use of your money.

Dealership operations are much the same. Now, I can't speak for all dealers and there is a variation between the margins for an RV dealer and a marine dealer, but the following are margins that I use when I analyze a dealership's business operations. Please keep in mind that the margins below are strictly my opinion based on experience and by no means represent industry standards. Anyway, having disclaimed my entire claim to fame, here's my input:

MARCO's MARGINS: What You Should Attain

New RV/Boat Sales	10-15% Gross Profit
Used RV/Boat Sales	20-25% Gross Profit
Service Retail Labor	75% Gross Profit
Service Warranty Labor	72% Gross Profit
Service Internal Labor	64% Gross Profit
Service Comeback Labor	0% Gross Profit
Service Retail Parts	40% Gross Profit
Service Warranty Parts	30% for RVs/10% for Marine
Service Internal Parts	25% Gross Profit
Service Come-back Parts	0% Gross Profit
F/I Reserves/Ext. Warranty	90% Gross Profit
	(10% allow for charge-backs)
Overall Dealership G/P	20-25% Gross Profit – in the black

RATIOS

Inventory Turns - RVs/Boats	3-4 Turns per year
	(Marine is usually lower)
Inventory Turns – Parts	6 Turns per year

When considering what you do with the gross profit earned by your dealership, the following guideline seems to have some merit (at least I think so):

- Dealership XYZ sells $5,000,000.00 per year.
- Gross profit is 22% per year of revenue; GP = $1,100,000.00
- From this GP of $1,100,000.00, you should spend the following:

PERSONNEL EXPENSE S/B no more than	40% =	$440,000
ADVERTISING EXPENSE S/B no more than	6% =	$66,000
FIXED EXPENSES S/B no more than	12% =	$132,000
SEMI-FIXED EXPENSES S/B no more than	13% =	$143,000
INTEREST EXPENSE S/B no more than	9% =	$99,000
TOTAL EXPENSES FROM G/P	79% =	$880,000

REMAINING PROFIT ($1,100,000 - $880,000)   = $220,000

NET PRE-TAX REALIZED BY DEALERSHIP   =   4.4%

I want to remind you that your margins and ratio may differ in your area because of environmental, economical, geographical, and political factors. Therefore, use the above only as a guide to develop a template that works for your dealership.

CHAPTER VI

UNDERSTANDING CASH FLOW – PART I

Where Did All My Cash Go?

As I travel to various states offering consulting services to RV/Marine/Auto dealers, they often request that I examine their accounting books in order to develop a report detailing their profitability for the year. Many dealers don't trust the financial reports generated by the accounting department or by their computer system, because the information appears to be inaccurate – and often times it is! One of the main things that disturbs owners and general managers is the fact that even though they may have been profitable for the year, they have no money in the bank - where did the profits go? The answer, of course, can be revealed by investigating the dealership's cash flow. Before we talk about cash flow, let us begin with a discussion of working capital.

How much wood could a woodchuck chuck if a woodchuck could chuck wood?

When a dealer is asked how much money he or she needs to run the business, the answer usually goes something like this:

Owner/GM Response: "Well, it all depends on the season.

Sometimes we need more cash when we are having more shows, hiring people, and advertising more and more. It just depends on a bunch of stuff."

Best Friends Consulting: "I realize this fact, but how much cash do you need to have in the bank on average in order to keep your business running smoothly?"

Owner/GM Response: "The answer to your question is very simple. We need enough cash to pay our bills! Our dealership usually has about $200,000 per month in expenses. So we need to have at least $200,000 available to pay our bills.

Best Friends Consulting: "So, how do you plan to get this $200,000?"

Owner/GM Response: "Well, when you've been in the business as long as I have, you come up with good ways to keep on top of this machinery. What we do is set a goal to get at least $5,000 per copy on each deal. So, we tell our sales staff that we must sell at least 40 units each and every month. We all know that 40 times $5,000 = $200,000. That's how we do it!"

Okay, now that we finished our questioning of the dealership top dogs, how would a knowledgeable Controller (or CPA) answer the question? They would tell you that to properly answer this question, you need to determine the average working capital figure for your dealership. Working capital is determined by looking at your balance sheet, taking your current assets, and subtracting your current liabilities. The balance reveals your working capital. To provide an example, we will now look at a simulated dealer's balance sheet and determine the working capital (by the way, we do realize that there are many more items on a dealer's balance sheet, but the below serves to illustrate our point):

Current Assets

- Cash in Bank	$75,000
- Account Receivable	$20,000
- Warranty Receivable	$5,000
- New Inventory	$1,000,000
- Used Inventory	$100,000
- Parts Inventory	$50,000
Total Current Assets	**$1,250,000**

Current Liabilities

- Accounts Payable	$60,000
- Wages Payable	$25,000
- Other Payables (Taxes, Etc.)	$30,000
- New Floor Plan Payable	$1,000,000
- Used Floor Payable	$20,000
Total Current Liabilities	**$1,135,000**

WORKING CAPITAL $115,000
(Current Assets – Current Liabilities = Working Capital)

The Controller (or CPA) looking at this data would tell you that your working capital is currently $115,000.

Now let's put the GM and the Controller (or CPA) together to have some fun. The Controller tells the GM that cash is at a historical low and that if cash doesn't get better soon, both will be out of a job. The GM tells the Controller he is out of his mind! The GM sold a record 40 units last month with a net of $5,000 per copy. He personally brought to the table $200,000 in gross profit

($5,000 x 40 units). The GM continues to argue that expenses for the month were only $100,000 and the net pre-tax for the dealership was $100,000. He reminds the Controller that his GM's bonus check was $10,000 since he gets 10% of the net pre-tax profit. So why is there a problem? What did accounting do with the money?

It is a good question, isn't it? Well, the answer can be found by examining your perspective. We will now look at the way both the GM looks at things and the Controller (or CPA) looks at the numbers.

GM		Controller (or CPA)	
Sales Income	+ $1,000,000	Sales Income	+ $1,000,000
Sales Cost	-$800,000	Floor plan Pay-off	- $800,000
Gross Profit	+$200,000	Trade-in Pay-off	- $200,000
Expenses	-$100,000	Expenses	- $100,000
Extra in Bank	+ $200,000	Cash in Bank	- $100,000
			(all time low!)

Digesting the Information

Can you see how the same information can be viewed in two different ways? Yes, the GM did have a great month. However, the cash profit went into used inventory as opposed to cash-in-bank. The GM had a wonderful month and the Controller had ulcers during the same month. You can see that both the GM and Controller have to help each other out. Cash can be increased in the above illustration by doing the following: 1) Wholesale the used units coming in on trade immediately; 2) Floor plan the used units immediately; or 3) Borrow the money you used to purchase the used units from a line of credit. Some dealers conclude that the answer to the whole cash problem is not to take trades anymore. We believe that trade-ins are the bread and butter of the business; why would you give up on a product that brings a gross profit of 15-30% on each deal? Even if you stopped taking in trades, what if you used $200,000 of your cash to build a four-bay service facility at your dealership? You end up having the same cash-flow problem. Do you conclude the best thing to do is not to build any new facilities?

So What Should a Good Owner or GM Do?
Best Friends Gives You Five Things to Consider:
   1.   First and foremost, understand how each deal affects your working capital. If it is a cash deal and you make a profit, then your cash increases. If it is a trade deal and you're putting the trade-in into your inventory, your cash decreases. Taking in a trade-in is just like writing a check on the spot to buy a unit from a customer. You gave him cash, and he or she gives you inventory. If you use your cash and convert it into another type of asset (parking lot, new building, computer system, company vehicle), you also will decrease your cash flow.
   2.   Establish a dollar value with both your Controller and GM as to where your working capital benchmark is to be placed. You need to clearly spell out to both of these people how much money you expect to keep in the business at all times. If your working capital gets below your benchmark, your Controller should alert you immediately so that the word goes out to the GM to stop taking in trades and making other major cash purchases until he sells something or other cash is secured.
   3.   Establish lines of credit for cash crunch situations. Many dealers try to negotiate a used floor or an alternate (non-flooring) line of credit with a local bank when things get tight. This is usually not a good time to negotiate with the bank. Establish lines of credit in advance so that you don't sweat the small stuff.

4. Provide training classes for upper management and the accounting manager on the subject of cash flow.

5. The Controller or Accounting Manager should provide a daily cash flow report to upper management. The report should list the operating bank account balance, checks written that day, contracts in transit (A/R), floor plan payables (A/P) on sold units, and lien pay-off (A/P) for use trades taken in.

CHAPTER VII

UNDERSTANDING CASH FLOW – PART II

Knowing Where My Cash is Going

Last chapter we discussed the matter of understanding dealership cash flow and answered the question, "where did all my cash go?" In this article, we want to focus in on developing a tool that will help you know where your cash is going on a daily basis. I have helped many dealers in the recent past, and I am always amazed at how both the large and small RV/Marine/Auto dealerships have not established a daily reporting system to monitor their cash flow. This oversight could cost a dealer his or her business! You may find yourself out-of-trust with a floor plan institution, or in an embarrassing situation in which the bank sends you those beautiful NSF (non-sufficient funds) love notes.

We at Best Friends Consulting don't want this to happen to you. May we make a recommendation to you?

The Daily Cash Flow Document

We recommend that the accounting manager produces a Daily Cash Flow Document that quickly informs you as a GM or owner as to what is coming into the pipeline and what is going out. The best way to discuss this helpful document is to show you a sample. Check out this three-page report:

PAGE ONE – Big Picture Overview (Summary Page)
Today's Date: November 17, 2012

Cash Position

1. Checkbook Balance - Operating Account	$95,000
2. Deposits Made Today	$15,000
3. Checks Written Today (see page 2)	-$20,000
Sub-total - New Bank Balance	$90,000

Results of Daily "Done" Deals (Sales)

1. Money Due from F & I Deals	$60,000
2. Floor plan Payable	-$75,000
3. Lien Payables (Trade-ins)	-$30,000
Sub-total	-$45,000

Today's Effects on Cash Flow (If Everything is done)

1. Cash Flow Change Based Checking	- $5,000
2. Cash Flow Based on Deals	- $45,000
Total Cash Flow Change (+/-)	- $50,000

Bottom Line Effect if Everything were to be received and paid off

1. New Checking Balance	$90,000
2. Deals - Contracts Income and Pay-offs	-$45,000
Real Available Cash...	$35,000

PAGE TWO – Checks Written Detail
CHECKS WRITTEN TODAY

DATE:	CK #	WRITTEN TO:	AMT	REASON
11/17/13	1402	JONES ELECTRIC	$3,000	Monthly Utilities
11/17/13	1403	RAYMOND THO	$1,000	Employee Advance
11/17/13	1404	OUTDOOR ADV.	$9,000	Billboard Advert.
11/17/13	1405	PETTY CASH	$300	Parts Dept.
11/17/13	1406	NELSON SMITH	$3,000	Return Cust. Dep.
11/17/13	1407	STAG PKWY	$3,700	Parts Purchase
TOTAL CHECKS WRITTEN TODAY:			$20,000	

PAGE THREE – Details on Deal
ACCOUNTS RECEIVABLES/PAYABLES - ALL DEALS

Date	Customer	Stock#	Contract	Floorplan In Transit	Trade Lien Pay-off	Notes Payoff
11/1/13	Robinson, Tom	P3434	$35,000	$30,000	$20,000	B of A
11/7/13	Franks, Bob	P2948	$25,000	$20,000	$0	DFS
11/9/13	Smith, Martin	P3948	$0	$15,000	$10,000	Cash Deal
TOTALS			$60,000	$75,000	$30,000	

Net Cash Flow Effect of All Deals: $60 - $75 - $30 = -$45k

Let's talk about the benefits!

The above tool is an excellent daily helper to you. The summary page tells you that as of today, your cash flow has decreased $50,000. It tells you that the accounting department wrote out checks totaling $20,000 and to whom they were written. While reviewing the details, you might find double payments to vendors, or items you had no idea were being purchased. You may also want to put in the order to "stop the checks from being mailed!" The report also shows that you only have $60,000 coming back to you from the contracts you mailed out, but you're going to have pay out $75K to the flooring company and $30K to pay off the trade lien. This means that if all the money you are expecting arrives and you do your pay-off, you end up -$45,000 in the red. Don't be fooled by your checking account balance, which says that you have $90,000 available; it is available today, but it will be gone when the day comes to do the pay-offs. By the way, the reason you have less cash coming from contracts compared to what you owe on pay-off is because on the Martin Smith deal, you had already collected $30,000 on 11/11/13 on a cash sale and had deposited the funds into your checking account on that day; that was a good day. But now you still must pay off the flooring and the lien pay-off. Even worse, if you get audited by the flooring institution, you will be considered out-of-trust because it has now been seven days since you were paid cash from Martin Smith and you have neglected to pay them off for the sold unit (you're in trouble now!).

The report also causes you to ask yourself, "Is it time to floor some used units or borrow some cash from my line-of-credit?" If you don't have used flooring or a line-of-credit, you may need to take some used piggies (used inventory) to the wholesale market. Well, mama always said not to beat a dead horse, so I think you get the general idea on what I am talking about in this chapter. The above tool will serve you very well and I recommend that if you don't already have a system in place, you should establish a reporting system to help you better visualize your cash coming in and going out. Please feel free to use the above form and modify it to fit the needs of your dealership.

CHAPTER VIII

WEEKLY MANAGEMENT MEETINGS

Successful Communication Leads to Profitability

We can learn a great deal about making our dealerships run efficiently by considering how we communicate our goals, visions, and strategies with all levels of management. When you watch a football game, you will find both offense and defense in a huddle prior to the snap. Why waste so much time in a huddle when you could be halfway down the field? Well, the football world realizes that it is absolutely essential to meet regularly in order for all team members to understand what the game plan is for the specific moment. The huddle helps each member to prepare for the upcoming play; it is used for brainstorming, for encouragement, and for correcting mistakes. The huddle only takes a matter of seconds, but it is so valuable to a winning team. What about RV/Marine/Auto dealerships? Oftentimes departments such as the Service Department or Sales Department will have their own departmental meetings, but rarely does the dealership have all departments meet on a regular basis (Sales, Parts, Service, Accounting, F & I, and upper management). What ends up happening in this situation is utter disorganization, confusion, and departmental competition. Each department acts as if they are in charge of the dealership, and the departments often try to figure out ways to promote the best interests of their own department. Salespeople tell technicians what, how, and when they should be doing something on a customer's sold unit. The Service Department figures out ways to charge more internals to the Sales Department. The Accounting Department is flooded with phone calls and visitors from other departments demanding reports, checks, vehicle information, commission checks, and they even expect Accounting to give them change for a dollar to purchase a soda from the vending machine. The Parts Department manager doesn't place special order requests for the technicians because they can't stand each other. Why is there so much confusion, disorganization, and division within a dealership? It can be summed up in two words: *leadership* and *communication*.

Leadership is badly needed in many RV/Marine/Auto dealerships. Owners/GMs must recognize that people have a tendency to want to do their own thing. Leadership must guide and direct the people, not vice versa. A good owner/GM should conduct a weekly meeting that includes all levels of management from all departments. If you're a small dealership, it may mean that only two people get together because that is the sum total of management – you still need to huddle together.

What Should We Talk About?

Having a weekly meeting for the sake of having a meeting is a waste of time. Here are a few pointers on what to discuss at the meetings:

1. Always introduce newly hired or promoted managers to the other department managers. Recognition is extremely important.
2. The GM or owner should lead the meeting.

3. The GM or owner should have a pre-written agenda that gives a brief recap of the activities of the previous week, provides information about upcoming events, and clearly communicates the goals of management at each meeting. Each department leader should be given about 5 minutes to discuss significant events taking place in their department and to share specific needs or problems that they need other departments to help resolve.

4. Use the meeting to praise noteworthy accomplishments by members of management.

5. Use the meeting to get managers involved in dealership problem solving (aging inventory, customer satisfaction, and marketing strategy). Brainstorming is a good activity that allows for ideas to flow freely, and it provides the managers with a sense that they are valued.

6. Use the meeting to provide training for managers. Managers are often leading and intellectually feeding others, but they often are not fed and will tend to become undernourished. Feed them, excite them, and educate them – they will then be able to do the same for their staff.

7. Promote interdependency at each and every meeting. Sales, Service, Parts, F & I, and Accounting need to be constantly reminded to work together for the good of the dealership.

CHAPTER IX

ACCOUNTING DEPARTMENT MONTH-END ISSUES

Month-end Closing: Do It Right! Always Know the Score!

In my travels across the country, I have seen dealerships that don't know if they made any money or not until months after the year ends. How can this be, you ask? Well, the answer is quite simple. The accounting department is usually running behind - way behind! It may be the month of April, but the accounting department has yet to close the books for January, February, and March. What this means is that the financials now become like a batch of scrambled eggs - running four months of numbers together like an omelet that contains ham and cheese (my personal favorite of course).

The Cure: Always Close Each Month in a Reasonable Amount of Time

We recommend that you close each month no later than the 10th day of the subsequent month. In other words, the books for January 2012 should be closed by February 10th, 2012. We assume that you realize the value of closing the books for each month in a timely manner, but just in case you've missed the boat, let me speak on this matter by sharing an illustration with you. Have you ever gone to a football game? How many players are allowed on the playing field? How many quarters of play are allowed per game? How are points given to each team? What services do the players provide the owners and fans? How do you know who finally won the game? Needless to say, each game has rules that govern how the game will be played and how to keep track of the score in order to determine a winner. A football game ends after four periods of play, unless of course the game ends up in a tie. Each touchdown is awarded six points, while extra points are awarded one point. A touchback counts for two points, and a field goal is worth three points. At the end of regulation play, which is four 15-minute quarters, the team with the most points wins - that's how it works!

Now what does all this mess have to do with dealership bookkeeping, you ask? Each month is like a football game to a dealership. The players are the employees who need to be paid. The number of points earned for the month are determined by the amount of RVs/Boats, service, parts, and F & I revenue you generate. The game starts on the first of the month and ends on the last day of the month. You can't go back and add points or take away points after two or three months. You win the game if your points for sales are greater than the penalty points you pay for the cost of goods sold and for dealership expenses. The final scorecard is presented to the owner/GM in order for him/her to evaluate the outcome of the month. Basically, the balance sheet and profit/loss statements are the two key scorecards management uses to figure out how the game turned out for the month. That's about all I need to say about the importance of closing the books for a month. Some dealers are totally lost because they either add or take away points months after the fact, therefore covering up or completely missing the true financial picture of the real game the dealership played during a specific past month.

How Does a Dealership Close Each Month in a Reasonable Amount of Time?

1. First and foremost, hire a competent accounting manager or controller; this is a key position in the life of a dealership, and it must not be overlooked. I have met accounting managers who have worked at dealerships for years but don't know the difference between a debit and a credit, let alone the distinction between a balance sheet and a profit/loss statement. Hire a competent person; nothing else is acceptable if you expect to close a month properly.

2. Ensure all departments have closed all completed transactions for the month.

> a. Service should close all R.O.s. for which the labor and parts installation have been completed.
> b. F/I should post all completed deals.
> c. Parts should receive all parts into the system which arrive at or prior to month-end and the receivers need to go to the accounting office ASAP.
> d. The Inventory Manager should conduct a complete vehicle/boat inventory on the 1st of each month.
> e. The parts manager should conduct a monthly cycle count (or a complete inventory) of his/her parts department.

3. The accounting manager or dealership controller should ensure the following takes place in the accounting office:

> a. All accounts payables for the month in closure should be posted into the system so that expenses and liabilities can be properly booked.
> b. All payrolls due to employees should be booked into the wages payable account.
> c. The floor plan accounts payable should be audited to the bank statement and reconciled to inventory on hand.

d. All accounts receivables and payables should be reconciled.

e. The parts inventory dollar value in the parts department should be reconciled with the balance sheet number.

f. All deals for the month should be audited by the accounting department to ensure proper posting.

g. All parts inventory received during the month should be posted to the parts inventory account on the balance sheet.

h. All RV/Boat inventory received during the month being closed should be posted to the RV/Boat inventory account.

i. The operating checking account should be reconciled with the bank statement.

j. After auditing all accounts, the accounting manager/controller should run a trial balance to ensure books are balanced.

k. Upper management should review a copy of the preliminary financial documents PRIOR to closing. Once reviewed by management, changes should be made as needed.

l. Once all accounts are audited and confirmed, a paper printout or electronic version of certain reports should be maintained on file for historical and auditing purposes (detail GL accounts, balance sheet, profit and loss statement, departmental reports, floor plan inventory, GL inventory, etc.).

m. A back up of the computer information system should be performed during the closing of the month.

n. You may now close the month.

Now, your dealership may not require all these steps because you have a small operation; however, MOST dealerships should do the above as a minimum. You might think that the above list is a lot to undertake each month. It is - and that's why the person in charge of the accounting department must be EXTREMELY competent!

If you notice carefully, most of the above routines really can be done weekly. The month-end process then becomes just a little more demanding than the usual week, but it won't be that difficult to close if you maintain a weekly discipline.

We encourage each of you to get involved with your accounting department to understand how they close each month. If they tell you they really don't have a plan of action, look out - you're in trouble!

Take care and may all your financials be prosperous.

CHAPTER X

COMPUTERING YOUR DEALERSHIP

The Time is Right for Going High Tech - Or Is It?

Manufacturers require it, owners need it, and workers can't live without it: Integrated Dealership Software.

So you're thinking about buying a fully integrated software package for your dealership? You've realized that in order to be more profitable and efficient, you must invest in the future, and now is the time! Even your manufacturers are telling you that in a short period of time, they will require you to submit all your warranty claims over the internet; you see the need for change has arrived. But which system should you buy? I have personally worked with IDS, Galaxy, Peachtree, Adams & Adams, Grapevine, Reynolds & Reynolds, and QuickBooks just to name a few. Each system has its positives and negatives, but which is the right one for you? Well, we can't tell you what you need to buy for your dealership. However, we can help you with your software purchase by posing a few questions that you need to answer. Let's consider these five questions:

Question # 1: What do you need the software to do for your dealership?   If you need something to organize the names of prospects for your dealership, you can buy a $100.00 or less product right off of the shelf at your local Office Depot store. If you're looking for a prospecting system that will integrate with your accounting, sales, F&I, service, and parts departments, then you will need to step up to the plate and purchase a fully integrated software package that allows data to be shared. Do you care if your system is operated in DOS, or would you like it to be Windows driven? Do you need a system that comes with a training audio/video feature, or one that comes with a training manual? Now, the questions that I have asked of you are pretty basic, but it will surprise you how many dealers buy the wrong system. This happens because they have not decided beforehand what their dealership needed. I have walked into dealerships and heard complaints from owners that sound something like this: "I purchased this high-powered server, several $2,000 computers, a tape back-up system, and a fully integrated software package for my dealership and I HATE IT!" When I asked them why they hate it, they said, "because it does a poor job tracking service R.O.s and the system has a poor parts inventory module!" If the owner knew in advance that he/she required a software package that was exceptional for parts and service, why did he/she buy what they bought? The answer is simple, they purchased something that "sounded good" but was not good for them. It is much like a farmer going to a car dealer to buy a good truck for the farm and ending up with a convertible Mustang; the Mustang is beautiful but it is not what the farmer needed. So, what does your dealership need in order to improve your operation? Determine this, and then you can specifically communicate your needs to the software companies in these areas.

Question # 2: How much are you willing to invest in your software purchase? Most dealers think that the only cost associated with installing a new software package into their dealership is the cost of the software - WRONG! You better be prepared to have an allocated budget to support the new software system your dealership is purchasing. Here's a little example of what I mean:

Dealer agrees to buy a software package for three terminals that costs $5,000.00 out the door. Now comes the surprises; let's look and see what is behind doors 1-6.

Door #1 - The dealer is informed that he will have to replace his current three computers that have only 1 GB of RAM with three new PCs. Add $3,000.00 to the surprise bucket.

Door #2 - The dealer is informed that his computers need to be networked by a "certified" computer network engineer along with the cost of CAT 5 lines, a hub switch, and a backup system. Add $2,500.00 to the surprise bucket.

Door #3 - The dealer is informed that he needs to pay a "special fee" to design his F&I forms. Add $400.00 to the fabulous surprise bucket.

Door #4 - The dealer is informed that his account has now been set-up with the software vendor and that he can look forward to receiving his monthly "support bill" of $200.00 a month to the surprise bucket.

Door #5 - The dealer realizes that he will get nowhere without receiving training for his people. The cost of three days of on-site training will add another $3,500.00 to the surprise bucket.

Door #6 - Finally, the dealer, fearing the future, answers the phone and is informed by the software company that he will have to install a dedicated phone line so that they can dial-up and provide routine updates and support. Add another $35.00 per month to the surprise bucket.

Friends, the above is not intended to scare you away from buying a software package, but you need to know how much you have to spend and how much it will cost you to purchase and maintain your system. Many dealers get mad with the software companies and they think, "These guys are ripping me off." In reality, I have found that most software companies charge boat and RV dealers much lower rates that they give auto dealers; Marine and RV dealers just don't realize how much modern technology costs. Bottom line: buy what you can afford and be happy with what you paid for.

Question # 3: Who is going to maintain your system on-site? Before you buy anything, you'd better find an individual at your dealership who can serve as the on-site computer guy (or gal). This person needs to be the one who maintains communication with the software company; the one who makes the back-ups; and the person who performs routine maintenance. If you don't have this person on-site, locate an affordable computer tech in your areas who will come at a moment's notice and who charges you a reasonable hourly rate ($20). Most technicians that I know charge $50 to $100 per hour, which will break the bank fast. When it comes to training, a designated staff member should be trained, and then he or she can train the people at your dealership. Otherwise, you will find the need to spend more money each time you have a staff change. The computer person you appoint should be an individual who is planning to stay with you for a VERY LONG TIME.

Question # 4: Do you know another dealer who is using the software package that you are planning to buy? Say you're ready to make a decision to buy; the next step is to visit a dealership that's already using the system and satisfied with it. Don't just make random phone calls to a list of dealers who claim to be happy with the software. Make phone calls and visit one of the dealerships to see the program in action, even if you have to fly from Florida to California to do it. It always mind-boggles me to see a dealer invest $90,000.00 in a system that he has not seen work effectively at a dealership. When you visit a dealership that's actually using the system, the employees will hit you with the truth because they use it daily. Take a day or two out of your life to call and get permission to visit a dealer so that you can observe and ask questions. It is better to sacrifice a day visiting a dealership than to be stuck with software you can't use for five or more years.

Question # 5: How long has the software you are considering been available to RV/Marine Boat Dealers, and when is the next version coming out? This is the last question to consider before we call it a day, so let's get to the point. You NEVER want to buy "proto-type" software or "vapor software" (software that exist only in marketing presentations but doesn't really exist at the operational level). If you find the software has been out for two years or less, be very cautious about buying it. If you learn a new version is about to be released with all the latest and greatest whistles, wait until that time (especially if what you need doesn't exist on the current version). Software companies are known for saying, "that's coming out in our next version."

Well, I want to wish you the best in your search for a dealership software package. Just remember, all software is a "work in progress," so don't expect any of them to be flawless regardless of the money you spend. Be patient with the software vendor and work with them; this is how you get ahead.

CHAPTER XI

DEALERSHIP PURCHASING

Who Does the Shopping for Your Dealership?

There is always that special person in your family who merits the 'outstanding shopper award'. This is the individual who knows when the specials are being offered and where to get coupons, and who is a master in the art of negotiation. When I was working in RV manufacturing, there was one key employee who knew every vendor in the county. He knew how to get discounts, he was able to return almost anything to vendors, and he knew how to control manufacturing purchasing cost. The RV dealership world, on the other hand, is a very different animal! Joe is in charge of purchasing new vehicles, Mary buys all used vehicles, Tom is in charge of wholesale purchases, Nancy buys all office supplies, Paul buys all office furniture, James purchases parts, Angela buys all computer equipment, and Bill is responsible for the sublet purchases. Now the situation grows even more complicated at multi-store dealerships, because they increase the cast of players. At times, it is necessary to have several people involved in purchasing, but RV dealers have a tendency to go overboard. The value of one or two individuals serving in the area of purchasing cannot be overestimated. It takes talented individuals to hunt for the best quality products at the best price. We believe dealerships should appoint a specific person (plus one alternate) to serve as the dealer's purchasing agent. If you have a small dealership, the selected person can do the job as an additional duty; in other words, if he is the F & I Manager, he continues doing his normal duties but is also responsible for purchasing. If you are a dealer who purchases $10,000,000 or more in parts, vehicle inventory, and office supplies, you really need to create an official position for a purchasing agent. Let's do some math at this point, because the argument will always be that you can't afford yet another job position at your dealership. If you purchase $50,000,000 annually in goods and you hire a talented purchasing agent who works on a base salary plus a bonus based on savings, how much value would this person add to the company if he or she was able to save you 2% annually? The answer is one million dollars minus their salary for the year. I am convinced that a two percent savings is attainable, and this savings could be sent straight to the bottom line through an organized purchasing program.

Benefits of Organizing Your Purchasing Practices

We would like to list a few benefits that may be attained through an organized purchasing program.

1. A purchasing system could be organized so that the Accounting Office will have a clear picture of the dollar value and description of items on orders. Vendors are notorious for selling merchandise to anyone at the dealership who will say "yes, I'll take it." When vendors recognize that all purchases require a purchase order (PO) to be issued by the purchasing agent, needless purchases are eliminated. When the end of the month arrives, the dollar commitment for new purchases becomes clear to management. Then they can establish an accrual account to cover these outstanding liabilities, or cancel orders to reduce liabilities. Keep in mind, if you have $200,000

in parts inventory at the end of the month plus $50,000 in parts on order, the end result will be that you will have $250,000 in parts assets and a new $50,000 debt.

2. Control of purchasing will eliminate wasteful purchases, which are generally haphazardly ordered by many people at the dealership. Additionally, this will prevent theft.

3. A purchasing agent is able to establish a good working relationship with vendors, and can thereby acquire the best quality at the best rate on a timely basis.

4. All levels of management will save time that is consumed daily by vendors who come to the dealership wanting to sell something. They all must consult with the purchasing agent who will quickly qualify these individuals and their products, preventing others from wasting time.

5. A purchasing agent can focus in on collecting rebates and co-op money from manufacturers as he or she monitors the buying and selling of RVs.

6. A purchasing agent can solicit participation from vendors to help cover advertising cost.

7. A purchasing agent can facilitate returning unneeded parts to vendors.

CHAPTER XII

EMPLOYEE JOB DESCRIPTIONS

An RV Dealer can improve the efficiency of their dealership overnight without spending a million bucks! During the past fifteen years, I have worked with over 100 dealers, and I can safely say that I have hardly ever found an RV dealership that has taken the time to write a job description for each key position at their business. I frequently ask employees to tell me what it is that they are required to do on a daily basis in order to earn a living at the dealership. Most of them tell me what they think they should be doing based on their time at the dealership. But when I ask them to tell me with 100 percent certainty if they are doing what their boss expects of them, that answer is a resounding NO because there are no written job descriptions. This being the case, it is very easy for employees to assume someone else is doing the job, and they love to blame others when things fall through the cracks. Can you imagine going to war with 100,000 troops and everyone is in charge of cooking, fighting, typing, equipping, training, and providing medical treatment? This would be disastrous and result in complete confusion and disorder. Believe it or not, this scenario happens daily in many RV dealerships throughout the United States. Everyone is supposed to do it, someone will do it, anybody can do it, but in the long run, it never gets done. Generally, when a dealership is looking for new employees, he advertises, performs an interview, hires the individual, and then puts the new person straight to work in a department that they may know nothing about. The person who trains them is usually a co-worker or the person who will be shortly quitting. The new employee learns by trial and error. The time and error expense are costs the dealership owner pays for through the nose. Why does it have to be like this? Well, the answer is that it doesn't. A good RV owner or General Manager must either take the time to write out job descriptions for employees or hire someone to do the necessary work. Job descriptions make life so much easier for everyone. Consider these benefits:

1. Job descriptions list most of the duties that are associated with the position being filled so that the employee understands what he or she is to do daily. This eliminates a great deal of confusion and disorganization.
2. Job descriptions can be used as a tool to evaluate an employee when the time comes for an evaluation.
3. Job descriptions are an effective tool to use when discipline is needed. You can show an employee the areas he or she needs to be working on in order to fulfill their duties.
4. Job descriptions provide a solid platform to build on, especially when you have multi-stores in your dealership. The same expectations will be promoted at all of your stores.

8 Tips on Writing Job Descriptions

1. Establish job descriptions for everyone in the dealership. If they are getting paid for it, tell them what they are supposed to do – don't assume anything.
2. When you write job descriptions, make them easy to read and understand.

3. Don't list every possible duty that could become a part of the position. Instead list the main duties that must be performed and then at the end of the job description, place a clause that states, "...and other duties as required by the members of management."

4. Make sure the job description specifically states who will serve as the employee's supervisor. For example, "The Parts Manager reports directly to the Service Manager."

5. Make sure each employee signs the job description at the bottom of the page, and then provide a copy for them to keep.

6. Type your job descriptions on a computer using software like Microsoft Word. This will allow you to modify your job descriptions easily as your needs change, and it will save you tons of time by not having to re-type things over and over.

7. Review your job descriptions annually to ensure that they are current and useful.

8. Involve department managers in writing descriptions, because they should know what needs to be done in their areas of supervision.

Sample Job Description

POSITION TITLE: Parts Manager

SUPERVISOR: The Parts Manager reports directly to the Service Manager.

OBJECTIVE: The Parts Manager is to supervise and manage the Parts Department (retail parts and hard parts), and the Parts Department staff. The Parts Manager's primary objective is to run a profitable Parts Department (maintain a minimum gross profit margin of 35% - retail parts and hard parts combined) on a monthly basis and to provide exceptional customer service and satisfaction to all parts customers.

DUTIES AND RESPONSIBILITIES: The Parts Manager will supervise the work and manage all aspects of the Parts Department. The Parts Manager shall ensure he or she provides leadership, which enables him/her to monitor all daily processes that include customer sales, internal parts sales, inventory control, parts purchasing, vendor relations, special orders, monthly/quarterly inventory, and pricing. The Parts Manager will ensure that both the hard parts and retail parts store are maintained in an organized and neat manner. The Parts Manager shall establish weekly work schedules. The Parts Manager shall recommend members of the parts staff for pay increases and will also take disciplinary action for employees who are performing their duties below standards; these actions shall all be accomplished both verbally and in a written fashion. The Parts Manager shall establish cash control procedures to insure that the daily closed tickets and customer payments are delivered to the appropriate individual in the Accounting Office. The Parts Manager shall establish a training program that allows the parts personnel the opportunity to increase product knowledge, sales skills, and daily operations knowledge including computer data entry skills. The Parts Manager shall produce a monthly report to the Service Manager that records parts sales revenue and gross profit for the month and compared last year's figure with the current month's figure. The Parts Manager is to make sure those bi-weekly payroll time cards and monthly commission sheets for parts personnel are accurate and submitted in a timely manner to the accounting department. Additionally, there will be other duties and responsibilities as required by management.

I have read and understand the above described JOB DESCRIPTION and I hereby accept the responsibility for performing these duties to the best of my ability.

_____   _____

Employee's Signature   Date

CHAPTER XIII

PROBLEM SOLVING – A MUST FOR MANAGERS

The military has been very influential in helping me compile useful tools for my consulting bag. I started serving in the Air Force in 1976 and I served until 2003 as a reservist. One of the most valuable lessons I ever learned was given to me at commissioned officer training school. We were instructed that the difference between success and failure was having the ability to problem solve quickly and effectively. The instructor taught us a six step systematic process to guide us in the heat of the battle. I am confident that if your managers learn and use this problem solving approach, your dealership will run more efficiently and profitably, and customer satisfaction will increase. An owner or GM will also find more time on their hands not having to resolve every little obstacle that arises.

The Six Steps of the Problem Solving Process
Step 1 - Recognizing the Problem

Each day a dealership will be faced with many challenging situations that require problem solving. The first and foremost step in the problem solving process is to recognize you have a problem. If your dealership is losing money or you can't seem to keep good employees on a long-term basis, then you must admit you have a problem. Life is all about change; in order to change for the better, you must admit you don't like the way things are going. In order to explain the problem solving process in this article, we will assume a dealer named Tropical Forest RV has a problem in its Service Department. Service has not been able to bring a single dime of profit to the dealership for the last four months. This is our problem.

Step 2 – Gather Data Relative to the Problem

In the next step, we need to get data before coming up with a solution. Managers have a tendency to recognize a problem and immediately come up with a solution without first considering the facts. Tropical Forest RV has ten technicians who are paid an hourly wage. A productivity analysis reveals technicians are paid for 40 hours a week but are only producing 20 hours a week; they are not on flag time because the new Service Manager prefers straight hourly wages. The technicians don't meet with the Service Manager on a regular basis. The Sales Manager usually gives daily assignments to the technicians because the Service Manager feels that the Sales department is more aware of what needs to be done. The Service Manager has been on the job five months now and everyone likes him because of his 'good old boy' attitude. There are no service writers, so technicians write up their own tickets. The dealership had a service writer, but the Service Manager did not get along with her. The owner has met with the Service Manager for the past two months reminding him that something needs to be done in the Service Department, to no avail.

Step 3 – List Possible Solutions

Based on the data in step two, Tropical Forest RV needs to

either train, reprimand, or replace the Service Manager. They definitely need to assign the job of Service Writer to a specific person. The work order assignments need to come from the Service Manager, not the Sales Manager. The Sales Manager can authorize internal repairs, but they should allow the Service Department to regulate its daily workflow. The number of technicians should possibly decrease based on the fact that the current ten technicians are producing only 20 hours a week. Technicians should be paid on flag time as opposed to hourly wages. Daily meetings between the Service Manager and the technicians will improve workflow and communications. The Service Manager was never trained or given a job description because he claimed to have 20 years' experience. Nonetheless, he needs a job description.

Step 4 – Test Possible Solutions

In step three, a variety of possible solutions were considered. You run all of these through your mind and you conclude that cutting back technicians is not the answer, because five months ago each tech was producing 50 hours weekly. Daily meetings would help, but the Service Manager should not have neglected these to begin with. The practice of allowing technicians to write their own tickets must be changed immediately. All in all, you hired the Service Manager exactly five months ago because he claimed to be an expert and a wiz at service, but the facts show differently. Additionally, he is not a person who likes to be given any recommendations for improvement; he believes he knows his job.

Step 5 – Select the Best Solution

You guessed it; the new Service Manager lacks the leadership skills and abilities to guide your service team. The best solution is to hire someone else for the job, but this time you will make sure the new manager receives a job description on day one and is closely supervised during the first month of employment.

Step 6 – Implement the Best Solution

You dismiss the Service Manager and hire a new one.

CHAPTER XIV

WHAT'S THE DEAL WITH THE INTERNET?

A Little Layman's History

RV dealers ask me questions about E-commerce on a daily basis. I address E-commerce in Chapter 15, but let's start with the Internet first. The magic of the Internet is that it allows millions of individuals to share data effectively at a very inexpensive price. I remember in the late 1970s how excited I was about being one of the first to acquire a Lexitron word processor for the military at George Air Force Base, California. The yearly lease was only $28,000! Later in the 1980s, personal computers (PCs) came out and the dream of many users was to own a machine that could process information faster and could share data with other users. PCs did get faster; diskettes, disks, magnetic tapes, and networking were a big help in giving us the ability to share information from one user to another. When the Internet became a reality, it was the ultimate answer to sharing data with people all around the world. All you needed was a personal computer containing a modem hooked up to an Internet Service Provider (ISP) and you're in business (now we even have high-speed cable – forget the modem). Sharing information is one thing, but then came the business folks who saw that you could make lots of money by sharing information, advertising, and most importantly by selling stuff on the net. If you want to share information, advertise, or sell products on the Internet, you begin by purchasing an address location (like buying a P.O. Box at the local post office) from a licensed organization that will sell you a domain name; the cost is about $10 to $25 per name (an example would be: www.rvcrofocala.com). After you purchase your own site, you can share data, advertise, or sell to anyone you wish in the world by constructing your own website. Before elaborating on what it is you plan to do on your website, we need to first consider the RV customer.

The Internet's Impact on the RV Customer

The main reason I use the Internet is to first get information and secondly to get a great deal on products sold on the net. I believe this same pattern holds true for the RV Internet shopper. Customers improve their product knowledge by visiting the manufacturer's websites, and they get answers from chatting or visiting newsgroups, which are specifically devoted to the RV world. After they gather their data, they begin visiting dealers' websites to shop for the best price – they're looking for a good deal! The Internet allows a person who lives in a small town to visit the biggest RV dealers in the country from the comfort of their living room or motorhome. They come to the Internet to see a large selection of RVs and to get price quotes (www.rvtraderonline.com alone has over 90,000 dealer units listed on their site). Many of these smart shoppers are saving big money by visiting a dealer's sales website on the Net. They send an E-mail to the Internet dealer to get a special price, and then they go to their local dealer to beat down the price based on the Internet advertised price of another dealer. This is done all day long and saves Internet shoppers thousands of dollars. Some shoppers even physically visit a local dealership, look at the units on the lot, and then get a price from the salesman. The customer then goes to that same dealer's website and gets a better price on the Net – talk about playing both sides against the middle! The Internet is also being used by RV customers to buy parts, extended warranties, tire insurance, vehicle insurance, and to finance/refinance their RVs. All of these websites save customers incredible amounts of money. We can't help but ask the question, "who would have made the money in the past by selling parts, warranty, insurance, and F & I?" We all know the answer to this question – local RV dealers, of course! Front-end and back-end profits are being reduced by the Internet sales. At first, dealers didn't think the Internet would affect them too much. They were wrong! Now people are finding finance, warranty, and insurance companies all selling direct to the customers, and every dealer feels the effects of the E-commerce world. If you doubt that the RV world has become this sophisticated, I encourage you to visit the websites listed below which allow customers to save thousands of dollars online:

Insurance– Vehicle Coverage

Farm City Insurance	www.rvadvantage.com
Good Sam's Insurance	www.goodsamrvinsurnace.com
GMAC Insurance	www.gmacinsurance.com
RV America Insurance	www.rvainsurance.com

Parts Sales

Camping World	www.campingworld.com
Arizona RV Salvage	www.azinc.com
RV Parts Outlet	www.rvpartsoutlet.com

Financing/Warranty Sales

Essex Credit   www.essexcredit.com/home/rv/

Warranty Direct   www.warrantydirect.com

There are literally hundreds of websites out there seeking the RV Internet customer. In light of all this, what is an RV dealer to do? Get on the Internet, of course!

CHAPTER XV

E-COMMERCE

What Should You Do At Your Dealership?

In the last chapter, we discussed the Internet and the impact it is having on RV dealerships throughout the U.S. In this chapter, let's discuss what dealers should do to stay in touch with the modern world.

Firstly, every dealership needs to establish a web presence. When the telephone was first invented, many were reluctant to buy one because they thought it was a passing fad (they were wrong). The telephone became an absolute necessity to stay competitive and profitable. What about cell phones, FAX machines, and personal computers? It's the same story; dealerships are finding that they must have all of these devices to communicate and process the paperwork required in the RV business. Eventually, RV manufacturers will require every dealer to submit its warranty claim forms and parts orders electronically. Because we are children of the new electronic market, each dealer should budget a small amount of money to set up a website in order to display its electronic store marketing catalog. You don't need to spend tons of money building a fancy 'e-commerce' site. Instead, what you need is a good, practical, useful, and economical website.

9 Tips on Establishing Web Presence:

1. Set up a website that displays your store, inventory, parts, service, rentals, directions to your dealership, and contact phone numbers. Pictures and videos are an absolute must! Remember, your website is your electronic catalog. When a person visits your site, they should get the feeling that they were at your actual dealership.

2. Market your service department BIG TIME! Believe it or not, you will sell more and more RVs on the net when customers feel that you will be able to provide for their service needs in the future. Service is the ticket to future Internet sales, so promote service on your site. I can't stress this enough.

3. When you purchase your site, always buy **both the .com and the .net** sites.

4. When constructing a site, make it simple. E-shoppers don't like to wait three minutes for pictures to appear when they first open your website; they are very impatient people. Speaking for myself, when a site takes more than a minute to load, I usually leave it and go elsewhere. The logic is that if it takes too long to open up page one, how much time am I going to waste looking at inventory?

5. Appoint one or two individuals to handle all incoming e-mails and telephone calls generated by your website. When you advertise on the web, offer special incentives which require them to contact these specific individuals in order to qualify for the 'special e-price'. One of the biggest sins you can commit against an e-shopper is to fail to respond to them within the first 24 hours. Your selected e-team staff can be sensitive to the e-customers' needs by providing digital pictures, e-mails, and customer support to the net shoppers on a timely basis. Don't give your e-traffic to just anyone! You must appoint a specialist; otherwise, you're wasting both your time and money advertising on the net.

6. Don't spend tons of money marketing your website. Instead, include your site on all business cards, billboards, letterheads, contracts, and flyers. You can even ask your RV manufacturer's sales rep to help kick in some money to assist you in marketing your website.

7. Don't throw out big dollars registering your site with dozens of search engine companies. You get more bang-for-your-buck by listing your site on places like www.rvusa.com or www.rvtraderonline.com. I sometimes hear a dealer bragging on how he is registered with 50 different search engines. So what?! Why spend this monthly or yearly fee to find 'maybe buyers'? I recommend you pay the small monthly fee to the sites I just mentioned above - they already have the buyers waiting to visit your e-store!

8. Once upon a time there was a dealership who built a wonderful site. It had terrific pictures, wonderful graphics, tremendous links, and an excellent database to search the inventory selection. The dealership even maintained a 24-hour hotline especially for e-visitors. As the story comes to an end, this marvelous dealership didn't sell a single motorhome on the net all year long! Why, you ask? Because it didn't offer any great deals on the net. Net shoppers are looking for a bargain - forget the bright lights and the 100 page websites. Offer your customers great deals. If you don't, your competition will!

9. Buy decent equipment for your e-business. Buy a good fast computer and a nice digital camera for your e-team. You can do this for less than $1,000.

Well, we'd better wrap it up for today. In closing, remember the e-world is a reality that is here to stay! Don't be afraid of it; instead, embrace it and learn how to economically market your products on the net.

CHAPTER XVI

CAPITALIZING ON THE CONSIGNMENT WORLD

Dealers Either Love Consignments or Hate Them

When visiting dealerships throughout the country, I have discovered that dealers either love consignments or they hate them. Generally speaking, those who are against having consignments on their lot believe that they are a headache for various reasons. These "anti-consignment" dealers claim that there is no money in consignments because the customer is usually asking too much for their consigned unit, or they believe that the condition of the consigned unit will make it very hard to sell. Another reason for dealers not wanting consigned units on their lot is that they believe that these units will be competing against their own used inventory. Finally, dealers don't like the fact that the customer will be constantly checking up on the sales status of their consigned unit; the customer is constantly reminding the dealer that he or she has to make the monthly payment, so the dealer had better do something to sell the unit. Well, we disagree with "anti - consignment" dealers and we encourage each and every dealer to maximize their profits through participation in the consignment world.

First, let's talk about the ABCs of doing business (i.e. - the cost of maintaining inventory).

Most dealers realize a net pre-tax profit of about 3% to 5% at the end of the year for their hard work at the dealership. Their entire combined gross profits from dealership sales (vehicles, service, parts, F & I) usually range from 15% to 22% depending on the efficiency of the dealership. This 15% to 22% GP margin now faces the task of paying for SG&A (selling, general, and administrative) expenses, which means that the 15-22% will now be reduced to 0-5% after all is said and done. Some expenses can be controlled while others cannot. A successful owner or GM has learned that expenses associated with new and used inventory must be controlled in order to achieve a profitable year. Consider the following expenses associated with inventory:

1. Interest paid to the Floor Plan Company
2. Loss of interest income because the dealership used its cash to buy used units
3. Insurance acquired to protect inventory on lot, especially for new units (required by floor plan companies)
4. Maintenance expenses paid to lot maintenance and detail personnel
5. Depreciation - all used units depreciate on a monthly basis and therefore have a lower ACV value the longer they are maintained in inventory (believe it or not, new units that remain unsold after 365 days will lose value also)

Now, let's get back to the consignment world. Do you realize that each consignment unit on your lot means that you have no interest to pay, no loss of interest income, no maintenance expense (should be paid by the customer), and no depreciation? You talk about the American Dream - consignments are a wonderful opportunity to increase dealership profits. You can make money when the consigned unit sells: on the front end, back end, administrative fees, and on the sale of parts and service. Not to mention the fact that now that the customer has sold his or her unit, they may possibly buy another unit from your dealership.

How do I Develop my Consignment Department?

1. Appoint an individual to be in charge of all consignment units. This can be a sales person, an F & I manager, or anyone else who is a capable individual and is already on the company payroll. This individual should be paid a small amount for each unit that is brought into the dealership's consignment inventory ($150). If the unit sells during the consignment period, pay the individual another small commission ($150) as an incentive. If the consignment manager sells the consigned unit himself, then reward him with the regular dealership commission. Explain to the consignment manager that it is his responsibility to ensure consigned units are organized and listed in the inventory report, and that he maintains constant contact with the customer whose unit is being displayed on the lot. The goal of management should be to develop the consignment department as its own profit center. As your consignment sales grow, you will need to hire additional people as needed.

2. Develop a service package specifically for consignment owners. Offer a monthly maintenance program that will ensure that the unit is maintained in a cleaned and washed condition for only $69.99 a month (or whatever rate you want to charge) . This will accomplish three things: 1) it will keep the consigned merchandise looking good; 2) it will bring in revenue to offset any maintenance cost; 3) it will prevent consignment owners from using the dealership lot as a 'parking/storage garage'. I believe this maintenance program will attract more customers as opposed to the program that some dealerships use, which charges a monthly consignment

fee without any consideration for the appearance of consignment units.

3. Recruit customers! The consignment manager should scan the 'RVs for Sale' section of newspapers within a 100 mile radius of the dealership on a daily basis. Individuals listing units for sale should be contacted by phone and told about the excellent opportunity to sell their unit at your dealership. Once contact has been made with the customer and he or she agrees to have the unit consigned at your dealership, have the customer deliver the unit to the lot and have them sign a consignment agreement form, which protects both the customer's and the dealership's interests. Before you agree to accept the consignment, make sure the selling price is not so out of line that it becomes impossible to sell the unit; the ACV value should be determined initially over the phone before the customer delivers the unit to your dealership. Another appraisal should be performed when the unit actually arrives.

4. Don't reinvent the wheel! Visit a dealer who is doing well with consignments and ask for his or her advice; better yet, go and visit that dealership. You may have to travel out of your local area, but it will be worth every penny of your investment. You can also call dealers on the phone to secure copies of the documents they use for consignment customers and to learn how they manage their consignment department.

5. Upper management needs to stand behind the consignment program! Yes, it is true that there will be no manufacturer's warranty repairs, internals, manufacturer's spiffs, special in-house dealership spiffs or ACV trade-in profits for the sales manager, but consignments will bring profits to the dealership. Upper management must support and promote the program; otherwise, the sales staff will just walk around consigned units.

6. Ultimately, reduce your inventory. The long range goal and benefit of an effective consignment program is to let the consignment owners pay the monthly interest, insurance, and maintenance expenses while the dealer enjoys the profits.

You can then use the cash that you would have put into the purchase of used inventory for other ventures and investments.

CHAPTER XVII

EFFECTIVE LEADERSHIP

Managing Your Personnel Effectively - Situational Leadership

The RV business challenges us in a variety of ways (inventory control, cash flow, profitability, recruiting good tech workers, and dealing with the world of technology); however, the area which consumes most of our time and expenses is the challenge of effectively managing our people at the dealership. I have met owners who rarely take a day off or even a vacation because they feel the need to be present at their dealership in order to remain profitable. They feel that without their presence, the dealership would fall apart even though the store has a Service manager, F & I manager, and Sales Manager working for them. What I have discovered is that owners have, in one way or another, mastered some leadership techniques and learned how to manage a variety of people. However, they have not passed these skills on to their management team, and therefore the team expects the coach to handle all major issues. This works fine for a little while, but have you ever heard the phrase, "get a life"? Your entire time will be consumed with dealership people problems. The joy of owning or managing a dealership will become a daily burden to you. Your management team needs to be trained in the area of leadership -

this cannot wait until next year. We want you to enjoy both your life and your RV business, so let us offer you a tip or two on this issue.

Resources – Who Can Live Without Them?

I have found that most managers in the RV business are very busy people who have little time to attend management classes at a local college or at a business school. Because of this, we must train our people at the dealership level. We need to offer our people instruction in management so they too can become good leaders and problem solvers. I highly recommend that you use The One Minute Manager, written by Ken Blanchard, as one of your textbooks. This book, which is available at most bookstores, is easy to read, thin in size, and written in a very enjoyable style. You can read the entire book in a matter of an hour or two. Ken Blanchard's basic presentation is that we must manage different people in different ways. One style does not work for everyone, because workers are at different levels of competency. Blanchard argues that we understand his four styles of leadership and then use them as appropriate with our people at the dealership. The book is so helpful because it reveals why you can't treat everyone the same and expect the same results. For example, you can tell a five-year old to crank up an RV and let out the slide, but the child will more than likely fail because he lacks knowledge and the physical ability to get the job done. Now, you can also tell a 40 year old man to do the same task and he could also fail the assignment because he lacks the proper competency to perform the task at hand. Blanchard's four styles of leadership really do work in the business world, and especially in the RV world! You really need to read his book. But in case you're not convinced yet, we can give you a quick little review of the four leadership styles that Blanchard developed so that you can enjoy this appetizer. But don't forget to buy the book!

Situational Leadership – The One Minute Manager

Managers are encouraged to remember that a good leader has various styles of leadership that he/she utilizes in motivating their workers. For your convenience, we have outlined Kenneth Blanchard's leadership strategies as described in his book The One Minute Manager. The four basic styles are...

Directing:

The manager provides specific instructions to his/her employees and closely supervises task accomplishment. Only the manager initiates problem solving and decision-making. Solutions and decisions are announced; communication is largely one-way, and the manager closely supervises the implementation of assigned tasks. Directing is the technique most often needed and utilized while training and instructing a brand new employee. Characteristics include telling employees what to do, seeking clarifying and confirming tasks, supervising closely, and following up.

Coaching:

The manager still provides a great deal of direction and leads with his/her ideas, but he or she also regards the follower's feelings regarding decisions as well as their ideas and suggestions. While two way communication and support are increased, control over decision-making remains with the leader. Characteristics include explaining the relationship between tasks and organizational goals, seeking clarification and confirmation around the task, supervising closely, and following up.

Supportive:

The focus of the control of day-to-day decision making and problem-solving shifts from the manager to the employee. The manager's role is to provide recognition and to actively listen and facilitate problem solving/decision making on the part of the worker. This is more appropriately used when the employee is more familiar with his/her job routine and responsibilities. Characteristics include asking for ideas, active listening, encouraging others to try their ideas, allowing others to structure the task, sharing control and accountability.

Delegating:

The manager discusses the problems with the worker until joint agreement is achieved on problem definition, and then the decision making process is delegated completely to the worker. Now the subordinate has significant control over how tasks are to be accomplished. Workers are encouraged to "run the whole show" because they have the competence and confidence to take responsibility for directing their own behavior. Characteristics include providing task boundaries; letting others make their own decisions; allowing others to chart their own course of action; providing freedom and autonomy; and providing help when requested.

CHAPTER XVIII

MANAGEMENT ISSUES - ACCOUNTING AND ADMINISTRATION

Keeping Your Dealership Healthy - Monthly Routines

Why do people get physical exams? Why do they routinely visit the dentist office? Why do we get tune-ups on our vehicles? You know very well why we do this: to prevent future problems. Many a person has been very thankful for routine physicals that have helped them find out useful information. The information allowed them the opportunity to catch a disease early in its developmental stage and thereby avoid serious complications or even death. I believe this same concept applies to the RV business. I have learned a variety of routines that I believe will help you maintain your business in good shape and avoid future complications. We shall now consider seven monthly routines that should take place at your RV dealership.

7 Monthly Check-up Routines

1. Reconcile your checkbook. Most dealerships have a main operating checking account for day-to-day expenses and a main savings account, just like we have at home. I am sure in your lifetime you have faced the consequences and humiliation of the NSF (non-sufficient funds) monster in your

personal life. Well, the NSF monster usually appears when we fail to keep our personal checkbook accurately balanced on a weekly basis. With checks, debits, ATM withdrawals, and the checking VISA card, you almost have to review your personal checkbook every few days to keep yourself balanced; this requires a great deal of discipline! The same is true with dealership accounts. I have visited a variety of dealerships that tell me that they reconcile their checking account every few months, or they tell me that their CPA does this for them. When I ask when the CPA reconciles their checkbook, they tell me after the checks have cleared and when a bank statement is available; this can only mean that the checkbook is balanced 30 to 60 days after the fact. Do you realize what a disaster could be inflicted on a dealership when you thought you had $75,000 in the bank and you really had -$25,000? Discipline your dealership to reconcile your checkbook monthly. Don't wait for a monthly statement; get online with your bank and GET A DAILY BALANCE AND CHECKS CLEARED REPORT. If your bank doesn't offer online banking services, switch banks! You can never afford to be in the dark when it comes to your cash position. When you're online with your bank, you can reconcile daily, weekly, and monthly. You can even perform balance transfers, stop payments, and perform deposit inquiries.

2. Reconcile Your Vehicle Inventory to the GL Account - a monthly inventory of units in stock compared to what is on the books is an absolute must. It is not enough to compare actual unit in stocks to your inventory report list. You must first get the inventory directly from the GL account maintained in the Accounting Office and then compare it to the monthly physical you performed. If a unit is sold or missing but money is still on the GL account, you have a problem. You might as well correct it now while you're facing the problem as opposed to later. The bigger the dealership, the greater the possibility of error. Once the reconciliation is

performed, file a copy of your working paper in a secure location.

3. Reconcile Your MSOs and Used Titles Monthly - if you purchased a new unit, you should have an MSO on hand. If you purchased a used unit, you should have a title in possession unless you floored the used unit after acquiring the title. Each month-end you should confirm both new MSO and used titles to your actual inventory. Produce a monthly report that lists missing titles each month and the reason why the title is not on-hand (awaiting pay-off, lost title, unit paid off but bank holding title, etc.).

4. Reconcile Your Floor plan to the Monthly Statement - just like you check your titles, check your floor plan statement. Make sure you are not getting charged interest for units that are still at the manufacturing plant, for units that are en route, or for units that are not in a sellable condition due to manufacturer's defect discovered at delivery.

5. Reconcile Your Parts Inventory to Accounting - every month, the parts department should produce a report indicating the amount of inventory they have on hand and the amount in work-in-progress. Adding on-hand quantities and work-in-progress together gives you the total parts inventory. Now compare this figure to what the Accounting Office has on the GL account - do they reconcile, or do you need to hit the Parts Department with an additional cost for the month? Save a copy of each month's parts inventory report.

6. Make a Monthly Back-up of All Your Data - every month, make a special back-up of your computerized data. Many dealers make routine copies of data; however, they erase past months to recycle their storage disks. This is a perfectly acceptable practice, but you should make a special month-end back up that you keep permanently in a safe place off of dealership property. If the entire dealership should burn to the ground, you would only lose 30 days' data or less, thereby avoiding a great disaster. Remember, making a back-up of your data and storing the back-up at the same location is convenient most of the time; but for hurricanes, tornadoes, earthquakes, and fires it's not so good.

7. Review Your Vehicle Purchases Monthly - produce a report that details all units purchased during the month. Believe it or not, simply knowing what you sold compared to what you purchased will help enlighten you in determining if you're going to have a cash flow problem in the very near future. Additionally, you will need to evaluate all used units purchased to ensure the sales manager gave them a 'proper ACV' value. If the ACV is off, now is the time to correct the error prior to closing the books for the month and paying too much commission.

Well, there are at least six or seven more routines to consider, but I think the above will keep you busy for a while.

CHAPTER XIX

A DEALERSHIP'S CHART OF ACCOUNTS

An Owner's Frustration!

I often run into dealers who tell me that the dumb computer just won't cooperate and behave itself. When I inquire further into this comment, the owner usually means that he or she cannot retrieve data from the computer to make informed business decisions on a daily basis. Interestingly enough, the owner is not aware that his accounting department is using a make-shift chart of accounts that has been designed by twelve people during the last four years. The reason the owner can't determine his inventory turns is because the accounts have not been set up correctly. The reason he is not able to determine how much of his service income is coming from internals as opposed to retail customers is because the only account that exists for the Service Department revenue in accounting is called, "SERVICE SALES." There is so much to say about a chart of accounts that time will not permit me to conduct a detailed discussion on this matter. What we can do is give you a sample chart of accounts for you to examine, and then you can contact us with your specific questions. Enjoy yourself!

The following provides an example for setting up your

chart of accounts. You as an RV/Marine/Auto Dealer can use this as a template for designing your own chart of accounts. You can change the template to fit your needs, of course. Please note that generally speaking, every REVENUE ACCOUNT has a corresponding COST ACCOUNT which is exactly 1000 numbers apart. For example, Revenue account 4000 goes with Cost Account 5000. You should always follow this simple pattern to facilitate your accounting.

NOTE: This is a simple set-up, but you can make it more detailed if you wish. For example, instead of one account called 'Advertising', you can make four accounts: 1) Advertising - TV; 2) Advertising - Newspaper; 3) Advertising - Internet; 4) Advertising - Billboards. The trick is to set up your chart of accounts right the first time; otherwise, it will become a nightmare to administer your dealership operations. Also, any chart of accounts that you set for your dealership should be blessed by your CPA.

Sample Chart of Accounts

GL ACCT. #	ACCOUNT DESCRIPTION	ACCOUNT TYPE
	ASSET ACCOUNTS (ACCOUNTS 1000-1999)	
1000	CLEARING - F/I	CLEARING
1010	CLEARING - WARRANTY	CLEARING
1020	CLEARING - PARTS AND SERVICE	CLEARING
	BANK ACCOUNTS AND CASH	
1100	B OF A - OPERATING ACCT	CHECKING
1110	B OF A - PAYROLL ACCT	CHECKING

1120	B OF A - RESERVE ACCT	CHECKING
1130	PETTY CASH - ACCOUNTING OFFICE	CHECKING
	ACCOUNTS RECEIVABLE	
1200	A/R-CONTRACTS IN TRANSIT	ACCOUNTS RECEIVABL
1210	A/R-CUSTOMER	ACCOUNTS RECEIVABL
1220	A/R-EMPLOYEE	ACCOUNTS RECEIVABL
1230	A/R-F&I RESERVE	ACCOUNTS RECEIVABL
1240	A/R-MFGR REBATE	ACCOUNTS RECEIVABL
1250	A/R-WARRANTY	ACCOUNTS RECEIVABL
	NEW INVENTORY	
1300	ARROWLITE - CUB - TT	NEW INVENTORY
1310	CHARIOT - PK MODEL	NEW INVENTORY
1320	COLEMAN - POP-UPS	NEW INVENTORY
1330	FLEETWOOD - TK CAMPERS	NEW INVENTORY
1340	FLEETWOOD - TT/FW	NEW INVENTORY
1350	XYZ PARK MODELS	NEW INVENTORY
1360	JAMBOREE - CLASS C	NEW INVENTORY
1370	COACHMAN – MH	NEW INVENTORY
1380	COACHMAN - TT/FW	NEW INVENTORY
1390	KING-OF-THE-ROAD – FW	NEW INVENTORY
1400	INV-NEW-OTH.	NEW INVENTORY
	USED INVENTORY	
1410	INV-USED MH/TT/FW	USED INVENTORY
1420	INV-USED-OTHER	USED INVENTORY
	ASSETS	
1500	INV- PARTS/ACC.	ASSET
1510	INV-PARTS SUBLET	ASSET
1520	PREPAID INSURANCE-HEALTH	ASSET
1530	PREPAID INSURANCE-PROPERTY	ASSET

1540	PREPAID OTHER	ASSET
1550	PREPAID RENT	ASSET
1560	PREPAID TAXES	ASSET
1570	PREPAID TRADE SHOWS	ASSET
1580	LABOR-IN-PROCESS	ASSET
1600	BUILDING AND IMPROV.	FIXED ASSET
1610	COMPANY VEHICLES	FIXED ASSET
1620	COMPUTERS & ACCESS	FIXED ASSET
1630	LAND	FIXED ASSET
1640	LAND IMPROVEMENTS	FIXED ASSET
1650	MACHINERY & EQUIPMENT	FIXED ASSET
1660	OFFICE EQUIPMENT	FIXED ASSET
1670	OFFICE FURNITURE	FIXED ASSET
1680	ACCUM DEP - BUILD/IMPROV	FIXED ASSET
1690	ACCUM DEP - VEHICLES	FIXED ASSET
1700	ACCUM DEP - COMPUTERS	FIXED ASSET
1710	ACCUM DEP - LAND IMPROV	FIXED ASSET
1720	ACCUM DEP - MACH/EQUIPMENT	FIXED ASSET
1730	ACCUM DEP - OFFICE EQUIPMENT	FIXED ASSET
1740	ACCUM DEP - OFFICE FURNITURE	FIXED ASSET
	LIABILITIES (ACCOUNTS 2000-2999)	
2000	A/P TRADE PAYABLE	ACCOUNTS PAYABLE
2010	AUTOMOBILE LOAN	ACCOUNTS PAYABLE
2020	CASULTY PAYABLE	ACCOUNTS PAYABLE
2030	CONSIGNMENTS PAYABLE	ACCOUNTS PAYABLE
2040	CUSTOMER DEPOSITS	ACCOUNTS PAYABLE
2050	DUE TO SHAREHOLDER #1	ACCOUNTS PAYABLE
2060	DUE TO SHAREHOLDER #2	ACCOUNTS PAYABLE
2070	EXT WARRANTY PAYABLE	ACCOUNTS PAYABLE
2080	INSURANCE - BLDG. & PROP PAYABLE	ACCOUNTS PAYABLE
2090	INSURANCE - HEALTH PAYABLE	ACCOUNTS PAYABLE

2100	LIENS (TRADE-IN) PAYABLE	ACCOUNTS PAYABLE
2110	LIFE/AH PAYABLE	ACCOUNTS PAYABLE
2120	MANUFACTURER'S A/P (PARTS ORDERED)	ACCOUNTS PAYABLE
2130	SALARY/WAGES/COMM PAYABLE	ACCOUNTS PAYABLE
2140	TAG & TITLE PAYABLE	ACCOUNTS PAYABLE
2200	ACCRUAL-SERV	LIABILITY ACCOUNT
2210	ACCRUAL - GASOLINE EXPENSE	LIABILITY ACCOUNT
2220	ACCRUAL-WRITE DOWN	LIABILITY ACCOUNT
2230	FUTA TAX	LIABILITY ACCOUNT
2240	SUTA TAX	LIABILITY ACCOUNT
2250	SALES TAX (STATE)	LIABILITY ACCOUNT
2300	F/P - B OF A - NEW	LIABILITY ACCOUNT
2310	F/P – G.E CAPITOL - NEW	LIABILITY ACCOUNT
2320	F/P - TEXTRON - NEW	LIABILITY ACCOUNT
2330	F/P - B OF A - USED	LIABILITY ACCOUNT
2340	F/P - B OF A - USED	LIABILITY ACCOUNT
	LIABILITIES (3000 SERIES FOR EQUITY ACCTS.)	
3000	CAPITAL STOCK-COMMON	EQUITY
3010	DRAWINGS	EQUITY
3020	RETAINED EARNINGS	EQUITY
	REVENUE ACCOUNTS (4000-4999)	
4000	ARROWLITE - CUB - TT	REVENUE
4010	CHARIOT - PK MODEL	REVENUE
4020	COLEMAN - POP-UPS	REVENUE
4030	FLEETWOOD - TK CAMPERS	REVENUE
4040	FLEETWOOD - TT/FW	REVENUE
4050	XYZ PARK MODELS	REVENUE
4060	JAMBOREE - CLASS C	REVENUE
4070	COACHMAN - MH	REVENUE

4080	COACHMAN - TT/FW	REVENUE
4090	KING-OF-THE-ROAD - FW	REVENUE
4100	NEW OTHER	REVENUE
4110	INV-USED MH/TT/FW	REVENUE
4120	INV-USED-OTHER	REVENUE
4130	DOC ADMIN FEES	REVENUE
4140	F&I INCOME	REVENUE
4150	CAMPGROUND INCOME	REVENUE
4160	EXTENDED WARRANTY	REVENUE
4170	TIRE GUARD	REVENUE
4180	PART-FREIGHT	REVENUE
4190	PARTS-RETAIL	REVENUE
4200	SERV-LABOR-INTERNAL	REVENUE
4210	SERV-LABOR-POLICY	REVENUE
4220	SERV-LABOR-RETAIL	REVENUE
4230	SERV-LABOR-WARR	REVENUE
4240	SERV-PARTS INTERNAL	REVENUE
4250	SERV-PARTS-POLICY	REVENUE
4260	SERV-PARTS RETAIL	REVENUE
4270	SERV-PARTS WARR	REVENUE
4280	SERV-SHOP SUPPLIES	REVENUE
4290	INTEREST EARNED	REVENUE
4300	OTH. INCOME	REVENUE
	COST ACCOUNTS (5000-5999)	
5000	ARROWLITE - CUB - TT	COST
5010	CHARIOT - PK MODEL	COST
5020	COLEMAN - POP-UPS	COST
5030	FLEETWOOD - TK CAMPERS	COST
5040	FLEETWOOD - TT/FW	COST
5050	XYZ PARK MODELS	COST
5060	JAMBOREE - CLASS C	COST
5070	COACHMAN - MH	COST

5080	COACHMAN - TT/FW	COST
5090	KING-OF-THE-ROAD - FW	COST
5100	NEW OTHER	COST
5110	INV-USED MH/TT/FW	COST
5120	INV-USED-OTHER	COST
5130	DOC ADMIN REFUNDS	COST
5140	F&I CHARGE BACKS	COST
5150	CAMPGROUND COST	COST
5160	EXTENDED WARRANTY	COST
5170	TIRE GUARD	COST
5180	PART-FREIGHT	COST
5190	PARTS-RETAIL	COST
5200	SERV-LABOR-INTERNAL	COST
5210	SERV-LABOR-POLICY	COST
5220	SERV-LABOR-RETAIL	COST
5230	SERV-LABOR-WARR	COST
5240	SERV-PARTS INTERNAL	COST
5250	SERV-PARTS-POLICY	COST
5260	SERV-PARTS RETAIL	COST
5270	SERV-PARTS WARR	COST
5280	SERV-SHOP SUPPLIES	COST
5290	WARR-LABOR-CHG BACK	COST
5300	WARR-PARTS-CHG BACK	COST
5310	MANUFACTURER'S REBATES	COST
5320	PARTS ADJ. ACCOUNT	COST
	EXPENSE ACCOUNTS (6000 SERIES)	
6000	ACCOUNTING - CPA EXPENSE	EXPENSE
6010	ADVERTISING	EXPENSE
6020	AUTO & TRUCK MAINT	EXPENSE
6030	BAD DEBTS EXP	EXPENSE
6040	BANK CHARGES	EXPENSE
6050	COMMISSIONS - F/I DEPT.	EXPENSE

6060	COMMISSIONS - SALES DEPT.	EXPENSE
6070	COMMISSIONS - SERVICE DEPT.	EXPENSE
6080	COMPUTER SUPPLIES	EXPENSE
6090	COMPUTER SUPPORT/SERVICES	EXPENSE
6100	CONTRIBUTIONS/DONATIONS	EXPENSE
6110	DEPRECIATION	EXPENSE
6120	DRIVERS EXPENSE	EXPENSE
6130	DUES & SUBSCRIPTIONS	EXPENSE
6140	ENTERTAINMENT	EXPENSE
6150	EQUIPMENT RENTAL	EXPENSE
6160	FREIGHT-PARTS	EXPENSE
6170	INSURANCE-HEALTH	EXPENSE
6180	INSURANCE-PROP & CASUAL	EXPENSE
6190	INSURANCE-WORKMEN'S COMP	EXPENSE
6200	INTEREST - FLOORPLAN	EXPENSE
6210	LEGAL FEES	EXPENSE
6220	LICENSES, PERMITS & OTH. TAXES	EXPENSE
6230	LOT MAINTENANCE	EXPENSE
6240	MISC. EXP	EXPENSE
6250	OFFICE EXPENSE	EXPENSE
6260	OUTSIDE LABOR	EXPENSE
6270	PAYROLL - CLERICAL	EXPENSE
6280	PAYROLL - DETAIL DEPT	EXPENSE
6290	PAYROLL - F/I MGT	EXPENSE
6300	PAYROLL - OFFICERS	EXPENSE
6310	PAYROLL - PARTS DEPT.	EXPENSE
6320	PAYROLL - SALES MGT	EXPENSE
6330	PAYROLL - SERVICE DEPT	EXPENSE
6340	PAYROLL TAXES	EXPENSE
6350	PEST CONTROL	EXPENSE
6360	POSTAGE/SHIPPING (NON-PARTS)	EXPENSE
6370	REAL ESTATE TAXES	EXPENSE
6380	RENT	EXPENSE

6390	SHOW EXPENSE	EXPENSE
6400	TAXES - CORP-FEDERAL	EXPENSE
6410	TAXES - CORP-STATE	EXPENSE
6420	TELEPHONE	EXPENSE
6430	TRAINING & EDUC.	EXPENSE
6440	TRAVEL AND ENTERTAINMENT	EXPENSE
6450	UTILITIES (ELEC/WATER/ETC.)	EXPENSE
6460	VEHICLE MAINT EXPENSE	EXPENSE
6470	WRITE-DOWNS (USED INVENTORY)	EXPENSE

CHAPTER XX

MONITORING YOUR TECHNICIANS' PRODUCTIVITY

The Future of the RV/Marine/Auto Industry - Service

Yes, you can get a good deal on the Internet when you're buying an RV or boat, financing your purchase, buying an extended warranty, and even buying an accidental death life insurance policy. But you can't get service over the Internet. Service is something every single RV and boat owner needs. The previous generations of RV and boat owners were individuals who enjoyed repairing their own units, but this is not the case for the new generation. They are accustomed to professional and prompt service. They don't want to get their hands dirty and when it's time to enjoy the road in their RV (or boat in the water), they want it to be ready as promised. What a difference a generation makes! When I served for three years as Vice President for an RV manufacturer, I cannot tell you how many phone calls I received from customers inquiring about where to take their units for prompt repairs. They were dissatisfied by many dealers' long waiting lists (two to four weeks' wait) or the failure of dealers to even perform repairs for customers who had purchased their RVs from another dealer. I believe RV/Marine/Auto dealers could once afford to say 'no thanks' to service demands by the public, but now things have changed. Because we believe in the future of providing service to the RV/Marine public, we will discuss matters that pertain to the service department from time to time. This issue is devoted to the discussion of monitoring technicians' productivity.

Do you pay your technicians hourly wages or flag time?

In providing consulting services to various dealers in the country, I find a large number of dealers who pay their technicians hourly wages. These dealers typically do not monitor the productivity of their service technicians and usually feel that something more should be done to improve their service department. Basically, when you pay a technician for 40 hours of work a week without monitoring their productivity, you are giving your technicians a vast amount of permission to be unproductive and you thereby reduce the profitability of your dealership.

We need to consider an illustration to assist us in our discussion at this point. In the spirit of keeping things simple, we shall assume you have only one technician assigned to your dealership who is paid $12 per hour, and he works at least 40 hours a week. Let's do the math now:

1 Tech x $12 per hour x 40 hours a week = $480.00 Weekly Paid Out

Now we ask the question, "of the forty hours worked, how many hours did you bill out to retail customers, warranty customers, body shop repair customers, and internals?" Believe it or not, many dealers tell me they don't really know how many hours are billed for each technician on a weekly basis. Well, let's do a little more math to illustrate the impact your technician's productivity has on your dealership.

HOURS PAID TO TECH	HOURS BILLED TO CUSTOMERS	HOURLY RATE CHARGED	REVENUE PRODUCED	PRODUCTIVITY RATE
1. 40	30	$65	30 x $65 = $1,950	75%
2. 40	40	$65	40 x $65 = $2,600	100%
3. 40	50	$65	50 x $65 = $3,250	125%

Now we want to look at what this means as far as gross profit goes for the service department:

1. Billed $1,950 for 30 hours and paid $480 to technician for 40 hours = $1,470 Profit (306% GP)
2. Billed $2,600 for 40 hours and paid $480 to technician for 40 hours = $2,120 Profit (442% GP)
3. Billed $3,250 for 50 hours and paid $480 to technician for 40 hours = $2,770 Profit (577% GP)

(Special Note: I realize that other consulting groups will tell you that the cost of technicians should be listed in your expense category under 'employee salaries' as opposed to your labor cost category. The net effect of posting technician's pay to the expense category is that it increases your gross profit in the service department. I simply don't agree with this philosophy. You need to know what your labor cost is for each billable ticket you produce. This is the only true way of determining both the productivity and gross profit margin of your service department.)

The obvious observation that can be made from the above illustration is that the more productive the technician, the more profit the dealer is able to attain. However, what is the problem with the above observation? The problem rests in the fact that if you were a technician, why would you want to work harder during your 40 hour weekly shift if you're still going to be compensated the same at the end of the week? It just doesn't make sense to work more and be rewarded the same. A smart technician can milk a dealer to death under the hourly wage plan. He will plan a day that will include doing a little bit here and a little bit there while ensuring routine smoke breaks and chit-chat sessions with other employees. Hourly wages simply promote an unproductive environment. We recommend you pay technicians based on flag time to the extent it does not exceed billable hours. For example, if a technician works 40 hours a week and produces 60 billable hours, then pay him for 60 hours that week. This means that instead of receiving his usual pay check of $480 (40 x $12 per hour), he will be compensated with a check of $720 (60 X $12 per hour). I can assure you that the extra $240 per week will definitely motivate your technician to be more productive. I have heard dealers tell me, "I can't be paying out that much money to each tech every week!" This statement is beyond comprehension to me; of course you can! The reason you are now able to bill out for 20 more hours is because that extra $240 per week you are paying your tech will come out of the extra $1,300 you billed out. What a deal!

If you're paying your techs weekly wages, we recommend you launch a test program with your most productive technician. Tell him or her that you want to experiment with the flag-time system - make the deal very sweet for them at this point. Tell the individual that you are going to pay them based on flag-time and as an extra incentive, you are going to raise their hourly rate of pay by $2.00 per hour for hours produced over 40 hours. In other words, if you are normally paying this individual $13.00 per hour, you will now pay them $15.00 for any hours over 40. The individual will realize the benefit of this plan and will participate with you. If all goes as planned, the tech will prosper and the dealership will also prosper. The tech will spread the news to the other techs and then it will be time to launch the program service-wide.

By the way, it is very important to have the service manager produce a weekly productivity report for the owner/GM of your dealership. You can't have the majority of productivity coming from internal repairs. In order to keep an eye on productivity in the areas of retail sales, warranty repairs, and internals, I have included the below spreadsheet. If you would like a free copy of this sheet which I have produced on EXCEL so that it does the calculations for you automatically, please send me an e-mail and I will give it to you free of charge.

Technician's Weekly Productivity Report to Management

Week Of: June 10-14	Name Brown, J.	Name Davis, R.	Name Johnson, M.	Totals
Retail Cust.				
Labor	22	15	30	67
Warranty				
Labor	15	5	15	35
Unit PDI	5	2	3	10
Total Billable	42	22	48	112
Internal	0	0	0	0
Time Clocked	40	40	43	123
Productivity	105%	55%	116%	91.1%

CHAPTER XXI

MANUFACTURER'S WARRANTY CLAIMS

Digging in the Warranty Gold Mine

As every RV Dealer recognizes, gross profits from the Service Department are a tremendous financial gain to the dealership. Many dealers charge retail customers an average of $75.00 to $120.00 per hour labor rate and pay out technicians an hourly flag time rate of $15.00 or less. A person can't help but to quickly recognize the importance of the service buck! In the above example, the bottom line results in a high gross profit ratio for the Service Department. What a gold mine! I am constantly amazed at how dealers throughout the nation overlook this opportunity without even batting an eye. I have seen dealers tell customers that they simply don't have time to perform service work on their unit. Instead, they refer the customer to another dealership or service center. My friends, with the arrival of the Internet, it doesn't take a rocket scientist to realize that front-end profits are going to drop dramatically within the next few years while the demand for service will continue to increase substantially. Just look at the car industry; without F & I and the Service Department, most car dealerships would be bankrupt. RV dealers need to embrace this reality and take advantage of the opportunity at hand. The Service Department produces its revenue, generally speaking, from three major sources: retail customers, internal repairs, and manufacturer's warranty repairs. In today's issue, we will focus on manufacturer's warranty repairs.

Serving in past years as General Manager and Vice President of a Class A manufacturing company, I want to share a reality with you. All manufacturers know that when units come off the production line, work still needs to be done to meet customer satisfaction demands. This becomes even more apparent the greater the delivery distance is between the manufacturer and the dealership, because things happen after the unit has been bouncing along the interstate for a couple of thousand miles. Cabinet doors may need adjusting, decals need attention, leaks may exists in plumbing areas, front caps and paint may get chipped, windshields may crack, front end alignments may be required, counter tops may need minor repairs, carpet or ceiling lining may have glue seeping out, and defects in appliances pop up out of nowhere. Remember, manufacturers expect warranty claims to be submitted by dealers, so why not take advantage of this opportunity? The one thing you must always remember when doing warranty repairs is to be fair with the manufacturer.

Warranty Suggestions

The best thing to do when receiving a new unit from a manufacturer is to have a thorough inspection performed by a specific person designated as 'receiver'. The receiver should follow a specific checklist in order to perform and record a complete inspection on every unit received. The receiver must always interview the driver who delivered the unit as to items that may be wrong on the RV. Drivers usually are truthful and honest people, and since they work for a drive-away company, they are generally very helpful to the dealership. If the receiver determines the unit has excessive amounts of defects that make the unit 'unavailable for customer sale', the receiver needs to report it to management immediately so that the floor plan interest is not paid by the dealership (the manufacturer should pay it). If the unit is marketable, the receiver should give a copy of the receiving report to the Service Writer immediately. The Service Writer personally inspects the unit and opens up a ticket on the unit as if a retail customer had delivered a unit to be repaired. Remember, the manufacturer is one of the dealer's best customers. Once the ticket is written up, the Service Manager should ensure that the warranty work is scheduled for repairs once warranty authorization has been received from the manufacturer. When the repairs are completed, a quick turn-around on the paperwork needs to happen by the person who files the claims with the manufacturer. When it comes to paperwork submission, this is where most dealers drop the ball big time! Dealers usually hire a person for low wages and expect great results – this is what I call 'stinkin' thinkin''. The person who submits the warranty claims at your dealership should have extensive service repair knowledge, be very familiar with labor rate manuals, skilled in negotiating repairs, and skilled in monitoring the warranty receivable account on a regular basis. This individual, often called the warranty clerk or manager, needs to receive a bonus commission based on the amount collected each month. This incentive will ensure you have a successful warranty claim submission and collection department. Keep in mind that you have already paid your technicians for their time; now it's time to get your return on your investment.

CHAPTER XXII

PERSONNEL – DEALERSHIP HIRING PROCESS

Hire the Right Person for the J.O.B.

Talk is cheap, so don't believe everything you read. Test your applicants!

If your dealership is typical, your personnel turnover rate should qualify you for some sort of crisis medal of honor. Losing an employee is bad enough, but I think hiring a new employee can turn out to be a real nightmare. You put an ad in the local newspaper clearly stating "experience preferred" and wouldn't you know it, every unemployed person in the city calls you assuming you really didn't mean you needed any experience to come work at your dealership. Then come the resumes from the applicants claiming things like "Bob has walked on water on three different occasions in the past," and "Mary requires only two hours of sleep - once a month." If these people are so great, why are they unemployed? Maybe they had a bad turn in their good fortune, or maybe they have relocated to your area, but how do you weed out the bad ones from the good ones?

We know the answer! Test them. It really works. For example, you need a data entry person for the accounting department. You receive ten applications and you want to begin the interview process. STOP. Before going any further, have a brief interview with the candidate, and if your initial impression is positive, have them take a "hands-on" test. Get one of your accounting personnel to give them a batch of data entry work and let them go to town on the computer. You can use a program like Microsoft Excel to test them as opposed to your dealership software so that it can be easier for the candidate. After about 15 to 20 minutes, examine their work, and you will be surprised at how many people can't do what they said they could do. Most people get hired because they *say they can*, but trust me my friend, have them *show you they can* and you will avoid a great deal of heartache.

If you're hiring an accounting manager, give them an accounting test. What's the use of hiring someone to be in charge of accounting that can't add or subtract? What if they can't tell the difference between a credit and a debit? You see, it doesn't matter if they have ten years of experience doing the job they applied for with your dealership. They may have been doing the job wrong for the past ten years. Please give them a test.

Now you may want to ask if the test needs to be in a written format. Well, this is a good question. I often give "verbal mental" tests to candidates. For example, if I want to hire a parts manager for the parts department, I will ask the person who claims to have experience to verbally tell me how the parts department works. He or she would respond by saying, "First I make sure that I stock the right parts for my tech. I do this by learning which parts are turning the fastest. My goal is to turn my inventory at least four times a year. I order my parts by locating the part name and number and then sending a P.O. to my vendor. When my parts arrive, I receive them and put them into my inventory through the computer system. I make sure my cost and sales prices are correct, along with my bin locations. Once I have received them, I put the P.O., receiver, and packing slip together by stapling them, and then I forward all my paperwork to the accounting department. The next thing I do....."

Now this guy knows what he is taking about. He can literally do what his resume claims because he is able to *verbalize* it. Another example could be the hiring of a sales manager. It doesn't matter that he worked for the largest, biggest, best, greatest, smartest, cleanest, dealership in the universe - as stated in his resume. What matters is if he can do a deal. Give the man a manager's inventory and then tell him to treat you just like a customer. Have him write you up on a worksheet and have him bump you a couple of times. Then let him do the numbers on you and give you an ACV on your trade. Have him get your signature and secure the deal with a deposit. Have him tell you about F/I and value of financing your purchase along with buying an extended warranty. Have him tell you about the fine service department and the excellent folks who do the tag and title paperwork. My friends, if the guy is any good, he will be able to sell you on day one. *Even if he doesn't know your dealership's systematic sales approach*, he should be able to do something with you. If he can't sell you, how on earth will he sell your customers and train your sales team? Test them and again I say, TEST THEM!

You will find that this method works. It will give you a good feeling when you find people who are capable and able to pass your test. It will also amaze you in regards to the number of people who don't know what they are talking about yet are demanding top dollar for their services.

Well, I want to wish you the best in your recruitment efforts. Happy employee hunting!

HOW TO
RUN A RV DEALERSHIP

22 Best Kept Secrets to Help You Run Your Dealership

Marco A. Martinez

Best Friends Consulting, Inc.

www.BestFriendsConsulting.com
Marco@BestFriendsConsulting.com

Made in the USA
Charleston, SC
29 July 2013